D1061287

The Arms Index (TRIN)

An Introduction to the Volume Analysis of Stock and Bond Markets

The Arms Index (TRIN)

An Introduction to the Volume Analysis of Stock and Bond Markets

RICHARD W. ARMS, JR.

DOW JONES-IRWIN Homewood, Illinois 60430

ROBERT MANNING
STROZIER LIBRARY

OCT 5 1989

Tallahassee, Florida

HG
4915
A74
1989

© RICHARD D. IRWIN, INC., 1989

Dow Jones-Irwin is a trademark of Dow Jones & Company, Inc.
All rights reserved. No part of this publication may be
reproduced, stored in a retrieval system, or transmitted,
in any form or by any means, electronic, mechanical,
photocopying, recording, or otherwise, without the prior
written permission of the publisher.

This publication is designed to provide accurate and
authoritative information in regard to the subject matter
covered. It is sold with the understanding that neither the
author nor the publisher is engaged in rendering legal, accounting,
or other professional service. If legal advice or other expert
assistance is required, the services of a competent
professional person should be sought.

From a Declaration of Principles jointly adopted by a Committee
of the American Bar Association and a Committee of Publishers.

Project editor: Jean Roberts
Production manager: Bette Ittersagen
Compositor: Carlisle Communications, Ltd.
Typeface: 11/13 Times Roman
Printer: Arcata Graphics/Kingsport

LIBRARY OF CONGRESS
Library of Congress Cataloging-in-Publication Data

Arms, Richard W., 1935–
    The Arms index (TRIN) : an introduction to the volume analysis of
stock and bond markets / by Richard W. Arms, Jr.
        p. cm.
    Bibliography
    Includes index.
    ISBN 1-556-23101-6
    1. Stock price indexes.   I. Title.
HG4915.A74 1988
332.63'222—dc19

88–17780
CIP

Printed in the United States of America

1 2 3 4 5 6 7 8 9 0 K 5 4 3 2 1 0 9 8

Contents

Preface

I would like to start this book by telling the reader of the many, many hours of work that went into testing a great number of possible indicators before arriving at the calculation of the Arms Index. In addition, I would enjoy relating the constant efforts which were necessary in order to convince the investment community of its validity. The lobbying and letter writing which were necessary in order to have it included in national publications and displayed on quotation devices would make a long and interesting story. I would like to do all of these things, but unfortunately I cannot. None of it would be true!

The truth is far more simple and far less dramatic. The Arms Index is the result of a fortuitous few seconds of intuitive thinking, based upon the observation of readily available information. It only needed to be made public, and it was on its way. I certainly was fortunate to have a few friends who recognized the validity of the index and insisted upon its publication. Wall Street quickly adopted it, and much to my surprise, would not let it fall by the wayside. Not I, but other technicians insisted that it be included in publications and displayed on quote machines.

Over 20 years ago I was a struggling retail stockbroker for a major wire house, trying hard to help my customers make money. By then I had already become aware of the pitfalls of fundamental market analysis and had delved into a number of technical methods such as point and figure and bar charting. This was long before I developed Equivolume Charting, however. I was probably more aware than most brokers of market measurements and indicators, but I was a long way from being an accomplished technical analyst. It was obvious to me, however, that my successful trades were very likely to be a result of buying at the right time and then selling at the right time, rather than a result of picking the right stock. Some stocks moved faster than others, and sometimes stocks did not follow the market, but it appeared that most stocks usually moved in the same direction as the market most of the time. Obviously, then, knowing market direction could be very helpful if I wanted to make money for my customers.

We had, at this time, moved into new offices, and had installed the very latest in quotation equipment. Rather than a slip of thermally printed paper which slid out of a slot on the machine, stock quotes appeared on a three-inch-wide screen, almost instantaneously! As I searched through the data provided by this delightful new toy, I came across some information which seemed to logically hold some clues to the internal condition of the market, and which, I thought, might provide some insight into future market direction. The information consisted of four different statistics: the number of stocks which were up for the day, the number of stocks which were down for the day, the volume in those stocks which were up, and the volume in those stocks which were down. It seemed logical to somehow compare these numbers and see if the stocks which were going up were getting their share of the volume; the result was the Arms Index, as it is now known.

I worked with this index for a few months, getting numbers from the machine and making the calculations on a slide rule, and the more I worked, the more logical the results seemed. I was then using the index only on an intraday basis as a short-term timing tool, and I found it was very helpful in knowing when, in a given day, to do my buying or selling.

I was fortunate at that time that the firm had as its technical analyst not only one of the best in the business, but one who was open to new ideas, Newton Zinder. I showed him the index; he immediately started using it, and encouraged me to continue to develop it. A few months later he asked me to write up the index and showed the resulting paper to Bob Stovall, who at that time was the director of research. He also saw more in the index than I had realized was there and passed the writeup on to Alan Abelson, the editor of *Barrons*. The article was published in August of 1967, under the title "Jack Be Nimble," and the Arms Index was on its way.

Since its inception it seems as though others were more aware than I of the usefulness of the index. I knew that it was very helpful to me on a short-term basis, and I was also using longer-term applications which I had not published. Soon, however, others started to use and develop applications of the index. Articles appeared in national publications and in many advisory letters. One of the first to use it was Richard Russell, writer of the advisory service *Dow Theory Letter,* who used a number of moving averages of the index. It was Dick Russell who first suggested the 21-day moving average to me, an application I still use. Soon to follow were others such as Arthur Merrill, Marty Zweig, Bob Prechter, and Stan Weinstein to name just a few.

Perhaps the biggest boost to the popularity of the index came with its inclusion on the major quotation systems. With this also came some confusion, however, in that each system gave it a different symbol. Whereas the *Barrons* article had called it the Short-Term Trading Index, Bunker-Ramo called it MKDS for some reason I have yet to fathom; the system which is now called ADP named the index STKS which is perhaps more logical; and Quotron gave it the symbol TRIN, evidently meaning Traders Index. The TRIN name became the most widely known and accepted. In fact many advisory services simply referred to the index as "the Trin."

It would be difficult here to attempt to mention and thank all of the people who have been helpful in recent years in the renaming of the index to the Arms Index. Certainly of great impact, however, was an excellent interview by Louis Rukeyser on his television show, "Wall $treet Week." Also, efforts on the part of Bob Prechter to have others call it the Arms Index were extremely helpful. I am indebted to the support from the Financial News Network, which has changed the print on their tape to ARMS instead of TRIN and which has allowed me a number of personal appearances on its interview shows. Bob Nurock included the index as a part of "the elves index" and gave proper credit. In addition, the support of the Market Technicians Association and its members has played a large part in the effort to standardize the name. As a result of all of the above, the index now appears as ARMS on most quotation systems.

With the Arms Index now so much a part of Wall Street, it has been important to include the thinking of many people in the contents of this book. I have tried to include any theories which are unique, but have, undoubtedly, missed a great number of methods because they just have not been brought to my attention. I am indebted, however, to the many analysts who have sent me copies of their newsletters which mention the index. Some of these people have been mentioned above, many are mentioned in the text as we look at their adaptions, and others who have lent support and ideas have been extremely helpful in trying to cover the major approaches to the index.

During the production phase of this book, the help of Phil Solosky and Charles Brauer was invaluable. Their computer expertise made the charting of data much easier and more accurate than the charts in my prior two books. Candia McNeal spent many hours in the library digging out data which then went into the computer. Afterward, her work on graphics was very helpful in developing a finished product. In addition, I am grateful to my son, Rick, for his work entering long columns of numbers in the computer, and to my wife, June, for putting up with an irritable husband under the pressure of a deadline.

Richard W. Arms, Jr.

Introduction

There is only one reason to buy a stock—to make money. Whether we are studying individual issues, as in my previous books, or the overall market, as in this book, those studies should be aimed at making better decisions. In the pages that follow we will look at a number of different approaches which are designed to do just that; help us to make better decisions and, therefore, to make money.

If our aim is to make money in stocks, what is more natural than to study price changes. If we own a stock and it goes up, we make money, so naturally we try to see the way in which stocks go up. Unfortunately, it is this reaction which has tended to make the study of volume lag behind the study of price. Another factor has been, of course, the traditional lack of information. Historically, one found it easier to get price data than to get volume data. In fact some foreign markets still do not report volume figures, considering the information to be confidential. Most markets now report volume, however, and the use of computers has simplified the application of that information.

It is our contention that volume is just as important as price movement in the understanding of markets. To ignore volume is to discard a valuable piece of information. We wouldn't think of buying a car without some idea of its power; whether it had enough strength to take us where we wanted to go. Why then would we buy into a stock market without an indication as to whether it had the horsepower to make us some money. Volume is a measure of that horsepower.

In the Arms Index, as in Equivolume charting, volume is made a full partner with price. It is assumed that price tells what is happening, while volume tells how it is happening. To look at either factor alone, not taking the other into consideration, gives an incomplete, and often erroneous, picture of the market. It is the partnership of volume and price which makes the index so effective. Just looking at the advance-decline figures can sometimes be quite misleading. One sees that more stocks are up than down and assumes that the market is, therefore, strong. Actually there are times when this is far from true, and the truth is only revealed when one looks at the volume figures. Then one may see that the up stocks are trading on low volume while the down stocks are trading on heavy volume. Under the guise of a strong market the sellers actually have the upper hand.

In the pages which follow we will look at the underlying picture which is revealed by the partnership of price and volume. We will study a large number of applications of the index, keeping in mind that different investors are keyed to

1

different time frames. We will look for a satisfactory methodology for everyone from the day trader to the long-term investor.

At times we will evaluate methods which we then discard, finding them less useful than others. In such cases we do so to make a point and to eliminate the need for others to cover the same ground again. We are not, however, engaging in mathematical experiments for the sheer pleasure of the mathematics. Our sole aim throughout this book is the isolation of the most profitable applications of the Arms Index.

We have attempted to cover most of the more obvious ways of using the index. In doing so we have talked to many other analysts and explored some of the methods they have relayed to us. This does not, and could not, cover all the possibilities. There could well be a better technique already in use of which we are not aware. In addition, there may be untried techniques, which will come to light at another time, that are more effective than anything in this book. Within these pages, however, resides the best thinking of a number of prominent technical analysts. Their results should help the reader to better understand the stock market, and, therefore, to make better market decisions.

The Arms Index was originally applied to New York Stock Exchange data, and it has generally continued to be used only in that context. Herein, for the first time, a set of new indices will be studied. These are Arms Indices for the Over-the-Counter market and the American Stock Exchange. These then are joined into an even broader index which we call the Giant Arms. In addition, we will see how these indices may differ from one another, giving signals thereby.

Another new application of the index is the Bond Arms Index. Here we will see how the same calculations can be used to help us to forecast the fixed side of the market, and, therefore, interest rates.

Methods of analysis are only useful if the investor has access to the information. In a later chapter we will cover the sources of data, both historical and current, for the continuing use of the methods revealed in this book.

The Arms Index is a very simple tool. All it really does is determine whether the up stocks or the down stocks are getting their share of the volume. However, its additional attribute is its ability to recognize those times when a move has persisted for too long and is, therefore, due for a correction. From that starting point it is only necessary to determine the best ways to display the information. Those ways are the subject matter of the pages which follow.

Chapter 1 Calculation of the Arms Index and the Reasoning Behind It

Perhaps it is the simplicity and logic of this index which has made it a part of Wall Street methodology. The numbers reflect the internal structure of the market and can help to reveal that structure without its being obscured by other external factors. Too often we find ourselves swayed by the emotionalism of the marketplace and fail to see the true supply-and-demand picture that is emerging. There are times when the popular stock market averages are telling us one thing while the index is telling us another. The index is showing us where the buying and selling pressures really are, regardless of the message being imparted by the popular averages.

We do not mean to imply that an average, whether the Dow Jones Industrials, the S&P 500, or the Wilshire 5000, is not a good measure of the market. It is important to have a useful measurement of the market, and we will, throughout this book, look at historical charts of a number of different averages in order to see what the market was doing at a certain time, and in order to measure the effectiveness of various applications of the index.

In its basic form there is no need for complex mathematics in the calculation and interpretation of the Arms Index. As we progress through the book there will be some use of more obscure mathematics, but all of this is a later development. Once the index came to the attention of market analysts, it was inevitable that each person would try his own refinement. In the pages that follow we will examine, compare, discuss, and accept or reject, a great number of these applications. In each case we will look at the formulas but will avoid complexities as much as possible.

This index owes its value to the fact that it is measuring the underlying supply-and-demand factors in the market. It asks if buying pressure or selling pressure is really controlling the market at any given time. By comparing advances and declines to the volume of trading occurring on those advances and declines it recognizes underlying pressures which are not apparent in just a price study.

The basic formula for the calculation of the Arms Index is absurdly simple:

$$\frac{\dfrac{A}{D}}{\dfrac{AV}{DV}} = \text{Arms Index}$$

Where A is the number of advancing stocks, D is the number of declining stocks, AV is the volume of trading in those stocks which are advancing, and DV is the volume of trading in those stocks which are declining.

Let us look at some real numbers. At the end of a recent trading session the following statistics were available. On the New York Stock Exchange, 974 stocks closed at higher prices than the prior day's closing level. During the same session, 642 stocks closed at lower prices than the prior day's closing level. In other words, 974 stocks were up while 642 were down. A number of stocks were also unchanged for the day. We will ignore them. On that day the advancing stocks had a combined total volume of 100,330,000 shares; while the declining stocks had a total combined volume of 45,990,000 shares. Again, there is another number which reflects the volume traded on stocks which showed no change for the day. This number seems to have little significance, and it does not enter into the calculation. Putting these four numbers into the formula, we have:

$$\frac{\dfrac{A}{D}}{\dfrac{AV}{DV}} = \frac{\dfrac{974}{642}}{\dfrac{100,330,000}{45,990,000}} = \text{Arms Index}$$

Carrying through the calculation, 974 divided by 642 equals 1.517 and 10033 divided by 4599 equals 2.182. (We dropped off the extra zeros in the volume figures. Since we are dividing, thereby establishing a ratio, we don't need the zeros, and they just clutter our worksheet.) So we now have a new fraction, made up of the results of clearing the prior fractions. It is:

$$\frac{1.517}{2.182}$$

which then divides out to produce our answer, which is .695. We usually round this off to two significant places, so our Arms Index for this particular day is .70.

This example, which yielded an index under 1.00, can be seen to have been a good day in the market. There were more stocks going up than going down, and those stocks which were going up were getting much heavier volume than were the declining issues. The index of .70 was, as we will see in later examples, a fairly normal and typical reading for this day. The S&P 500 stock average for the day advanced 1.88 points, and the Dow Industrials were up over 25 points.

A closer look at these numbers can help us to understand the nature of the index. The first fraction, the advances and declines, shows us that there were over 1.5 stocks going up for every one stock going down, therefore, the value of 1.517. This is, in itself, an impressive number, reflecting a strong market move. The second fraction produces a value of 2.182, however, which is even more impressive. There were more than two shares traded on the upside for each share traded on the downside. We see, then, that the stocks which were going up were getting more than their share of the volume. This produced the index of .70. *Indices which are under 1.00 are bullish.*

For a second example let us look at a less bullish situation. These numbers came from readings taken in the middle of a trading day, rather than at the close of the day's trading. The index can be calculated as often as desired, since the component numbers are constantly updated on most quotation devices throughout the trading day. In fact, the computations we are now studying are usually unnecessary, since the index is computed and displayed on most quote machines and crosses the tape on the Financial News Network, recalculated every minute or two.

At noon, New York time, 660 stocks are registering advances while 858 are registering declines. So far in the day, 15,120,000 shares have traded in those stocks which are showing advances, while 26,030,000 shares have traded in those stocks showing declines. The computation then:

$$\cfrac{\cfrac{A}{D}}{\cfrac{AD}{DV}} = \cfrac{\cfrac{660}{858}}{\cfrac{1512}{2603}} = \cfrac{.769}{.581} = 1.32$$

So, the Arms Index at that instant is 1.32. It can (and will) change throughout the trading day, and the interpretation of those changes will be the subject of our next chapter. This reading, being over 1.00, is a bearish reading. The declining stocks are receiving more than their share of the volume. The first fraction, which compares advances to declines, indicates with its .769 value that about 1.3 companies are trading on the downside for every company trading on the upside (1.3 is the reciprocal of .769). This is, in itself, a statistic which indicates the market is under pressure, so we would expect a bearish reading for the index. The second fraction does, in fact, confirm this expectation, giving a reading of .581. It is telling us that 1.72 shares are trading on the upside for every share trading on the downside (as above, using the reciprocal of .581, which is 1.72). Consequently, the index gives us a value which we would expect and consider normal at this time: 1.32. *An index over 1.00 is considered a bearish reading.*

So far we have looked at examples which are quite normal, with a low index during an advance and a high index during a decline. Such will not always be the case, luckily, since it is the unusual action which can impart valuable information; information which can lead to stock market profits.

Let us look at a more unusual index and try to understand what the numbers are saying. On May 1, 1986, at the close, the following numbers were seen:

Advances 623
Declines 980
Advancing Volume 59,610,000
Declining Volume 69,200,000
Therefore:

$$\cfrac{\cfrac{623}{980}}{\cfrac{5961}{6920}} = \cfrac{.636}{.861} = .74$$

So, we are looking at a day in which there are many more stocks down than up, and there is a far smaller discrepancy when we are looking at the advancing and declining volume figures. A person watching just the advance-decline relationship would assume this was a bad day in the market; more stocks were down than were up. Even a person observing only the advancing and declining volume would reach the same conclusion; volume was heavier on the downside than on the upside. However, the Arms Index imparted a rather different message. It pointed out that although the advances were behind declines and advancing volume was behind declining volume, the down stocks did not receive their share of the volume. Those fewer advancing issues were receiving proportionately more than their share of the volume. In the guise of a down day, (the averages were also somewhat lower) buying was moving into the marketplace. This reading on the index was a warning that the market was actually stronger than the averages were implying.

As our last example let us look at another unusual day, but this time an advancing day. On May 13, 1983, at the end of the trading day, the following statistics were posted:

Advances 1056

Declines 545

Advancing Volume 48,490,000

Declining Volume 25,070,000

So the calculation would go as follows:

$$\frac{\dfrac{1056}{545}}{\dfrac{4849}{2507}} = \frac{1.94}{1.93} = 1.01$$

Here we see that advances lead declines by almost a two-to-one margin. We would construe that as being a rather strong day if we were looking only at that statistic. Looking at the upside and downside volume figures, we see that they also appear strong; as with the prior fraction a two-to-one ratio. However, since both ratios are almost identical we come up with an Arms Index of 1.01, which is not at all bullish, and is, in fact, just barely on the bearish side.

During the above trading day the S&P 500 Stock Index moved upward over one-half a point, confirming the apparent strength of the day. The Arms Index was telling us more, however, It was saying that the apparent strength lost some credibility because it was not sustained by the index. Under the guise of a strong market, buyers were selling quite a bit of stock; enough to push the index across to bearish territory.

It should be understood that a single day such as either of the above does not in itself carry so much significance as to forecast a major turn in the market. It does, however, serve as a warning and plays a part in longer-term forecasting when accompanied by other days of the same genre. In later chapters these days will become significant as we see how they tend to swing moving averages for us.

As we have seen, a neutral index is 1.00 so we would also expect that the average index, or normal level of the index, should be 1.00. We averaged the values of the index on a closing basis for a 10-year period to see if this is true. Interestingly, the result showed the index to average slightly in bearish territory at 1.02827 for this period, a time span that encompassed both bull and bear markets and which ended close to the level where it began. The reason would seem to be that the index is restricted between zero and one on the bullish side, but is open-ended, going, theoretically, from one to infinity on the bearish side. In a later section we will look more closely at this fact and study some ways to correct for it. For our present discussion, however, it is not necessary to be concerned with this discrepancy. The index does have a normal level very close to 1.00.

Figure 1–1 shows the values of the Arms Index for the first three months of 1985. The first day of the year was very bearish, with an index reading over 2.60, but the rest of the data indicates that most days were fairly close to the 1.00 level. The lowest reading was under .40 and was also a relatively rare occurrence. There appears to be a tendency for readings below 1.00 which may reflect that the market was advancing during these three months.

Prior to the market panic of October 1987, the highest closing indices never reached 5.00 and any reading over 2.50 was considered extremely bearish. The numbers generated in the panic were over 10.00 on two different days, producing anomalies never seen before. On the bullish side, any readings under .40 are very unusual on a closing basis and reflect extremely strong conditions. Rarely, is a closing index under .30 seen.

Figure 1–2 is a scatter chart of the index over a three-year period. More than 750 data points have been entered, each representing the level of the index and the

Figure 1–1

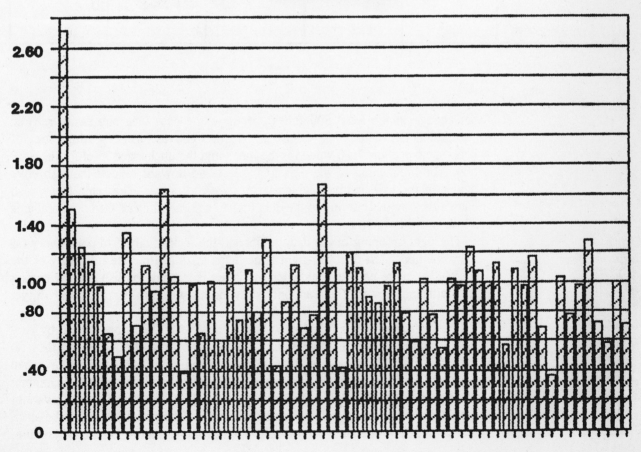

1985 JAN THRU MAR

NYSE ARMS INDEX

Figure 1–2

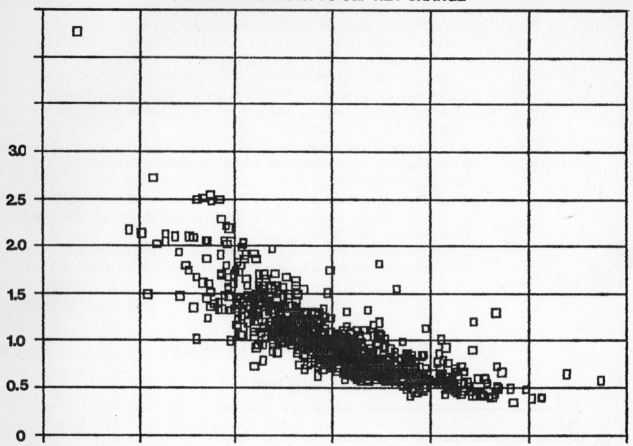

NYSE ARMS INDEX VS S&P NET CHANGE

net change in the S&P 500 Index for the same day. One can easily see the correlation between index values and market moves. Most postings are, of course, close to the 1.00 value for the index and the unchanged level for the S&P 500. The broadening of the data to the left and upward reflects the restrictive nature of the low numbers which we referred to above. The same factor also causes the obvious curving of the data toward a parallelling of the horizontal axis as we move to the right.

The tight grouping of the data points and the lack of any data points very far from the upper-left to lower-right zone helps to dramatize the reliability of the index. There are no instances when the index is strongly bullish and the market is significantly lower. There are only a few points where the index is bearish, yet the market posts a worthwhile gain.

The question is often asked as to how to deal with distortions caused by very heavy trading in one or more stocks. These distortions do occur, and they do effect the index. This is especially true near the beginning of the trading day when a large block in an issue can have a noticeable effect by allocating a large amount of volume to either the plus side or the minus side. Our answer is to be aware of the distortions, but not to try to correct for them. The volume is real—the stock really traded, so it cannot be subtracted out of the equation. On the other hand, the distortion could throw off the judgement of the short-term trader, so he should realize the distortion is present. As the day progresses the distortion is likely to become less important as volume builds in other issues. When we are dealing with longer-term indices these distortions are inconsequential, whereas to have subtracted the numbers from the market would mean we were dealing with an inaccurate picture of history.

We should be aware that the index is providing a mathematical, almost mechanical, method for viewing the marketplace. We should not, however, lose sight of the fact that human emotions are being measured, and it is those human emotions which are the true force behind market movement. When the index is giving low readings, which we interpret as bullish, it is reflecting the actions of people; people who are spending precious dollars to buy stocks. The bullish reading is produced because the buyers are aggressively moving into the marketplace. They are producing unusually heavy volume in those stocks which are going up, and they are doing proportionately less trading in the stocks which are declining.

When the index is exhibiting a high number, we say that it is bearish. In reality, it is reflecting a fearful attitude on the part of a majority of traders. They are selling heavily; thereby producing more volume in the stocks which are declining. Stock prices move upward or downward in response to emotions. Undoubtedly, there are fundamental factors which are affecting the public's emotions, but is it the interpretation of those facts, rather than the facts themselves, which move prices and create volume? If the interpretation of those facts generates a fearful attitude, people will put pressure on the sell side of the market. This creates volume in the declining issues, which thereby produces a high reading in the index; a bearish reading.

Actually, since there are four variables in the index, there are four factors which can effect its value. A reading can become more bullish if there is a decrease in the number of advancing issues, for example, while the other three factors remain relatively unchanged. This means that the volume traded on the upside is being concentrated in fewer stocks, so those stocks are getting more than their share of the volume. At first glance it seems illogical that a decrease in advances would be bullish, but upon reflection we see that those stocks which have left the advance list are light traders, while those which have remained on the advance list are heavy traders. In reality, this is showing us a bullish scenario. People are continuing to put their money into the few stocks which are up, creating heavy volume in those issues.

A similar shift to the bullish side could be caused by an increase in the number of declining issues without a similar increase in declining volume. In this case, the stocks which have moved to the minus side are evidently light traders. The heavy traders are remaining on the plus side. The index is evaluating the emotions present in the marketplace, seeing that the preponderance of volume is being concentrated in those stocks which are up, and giving us a bullish reading.

The third and fourth cases are more easily understood. A sharp increase in upside volume without any great change in the other three factors reflects a move by the public to pour their money into those stocks which are already showing advances. It is obviously a bullish sign; traders are aggressively moving into popular issues. Similarly, a decrease in downside volume indicates a public abandonment of the sell side. They are no longer as aggressively liquidating, so the index reflects this change in emotions by giving us a more bullish reading.

In reality, all four of the numbers are likely to be changing throughout the trading day, thereby reflecting the four factors simultaneously. Of course, the above interpretation is equally true in the other direction as index readings become more bearish.

We have now seen how the index is calculated, and have been able to get some idea of its normal range, its extremes, and its anomalies. In the next chapter we will put this information to work in the marketplace, seeing how it can be helpful in short-term timing.

Chapter 2 Intraday Uses of the Arms Index

As will be seen, the ways of using the Arms Index are myriad and range from short-term to long-term applications. We will deal first with the simplest and most immediate uses of the index, attempting to identify methods of better timing our stock market activity. As will be true throughout the chapters that follow, we will explore the use of the index with one aim in mind; better market decisions. The first consideration, then, is the use of the index for relatively short time spans. Later we will search for applications which will help our longer-term market decisions.

The original development of this index was done in order to try to understand the intraday gyrations of the market. It was only later that many people (including the author) began to work with smoothing techniques, applied to closing index values, in order to predict longer-term market moves. The longer-term work has become so popular, however, that many analysts have forgotten the original reason for the index; the recognition of intraday changes of direction. Yet, this function is useful and important.

Because of the index's genesis as an intraday tool it was originally, and perhaps unfortunately, named the Short-Term Trading Index. This has often scared off investors whose immediate response was: "That's not for me, I'm an investor not a trader!" Yet every market participant, be he a trader or a long-term investor, must at some time enter the marketplace with his bundle and lay it on the line. At that time it really does not matter whether or not he is a short-term trader. He is still, through his broker on the floor of the exchange, participating in a market where prices can move very rapidly minute to minute throughout the trading day. Consequently, timing can still make a difference of many dollars; real dollars with the same value to the investor as to the trader.

The short-term trader, especially the day trader, does not have the luxury of waiting. His decisions must be made in the context of the current market. For him the Arms Index can be an extremely valuable tool allowing him to recognize, as quickly as possible, the schizophrenic mood changes as they sweep through the trading crowd. His survival depends upon his ability to sense those shifts of emotion and act decisively. It is perhaps for this reason that the current value of the index is prominently displayed on video screens at so many trading posts on so many different exchanges.

The longer-term investor is in a less vulnerable position because he does have the luxury of waiting. Having decided to buy a particular stock, he can then do so at a time which he believes to be opportune. Yet, most longer-term stock buyers fail to take advantage of that luxury. Having decided to buy a stock, they proceed to blindly step in and buy it, regardless of the market. Their rationalization is the assertion that they should not be concerned with small price moves because they are in for "the long pull" and fractions are of little consequence. Often the truth behind their rationale is that they do not understand the short-term market and feel unable to time their transactions, so they randomly place their orders, hoping for a good price.

The Arms Index can help both of these groups. It allows an insight into the changing psychology of the trading crowd, often giving signals before they become apparent in the market averages. For the trader it can mean the difference of fractions of a point as he reacts to changes of market direction. To the investor it can mean the difference between buying now or waiting until later in the day when prices may be lower.

The index is constantly changing throughout the trading day, and those changes are easily accessible. Most quote machines in brokerage offices carry the index and update it every minute. The symbol has recently been changed on both the ADP system and the Bunker-Ramo system to ARMS from the prior symbols which were STKS and MKDS respectively. The Bunker-Ramo display is particularly helpful because, in addition to showing the up-to-the-minute index, the values at the end of each trading hour are retained and presented in an easily scanned format. On the Quotron equipment the symbol is TRIN which was derived from the original name of the index, the TRaders INdex. It was this symbol which was popularized by many market writers who started calling the index "the Trin."

Those who watch the market on their television sets are able to constantly monitor the index as it crosses the tape. The Financial News Network, thanks to the efforts of its technical analyst, John Bollinger, identifies the index by the symbol ARMS while others still use the name TRIN. Whichever symbol is used, however, it is the same index, calculated in the same way.

In using the index during a single trading day there are two considerations which are important; the value of the index, and the way in which the index is changing. Both impart useful information, and neither should be ignored. In addition, the value of the index is enhanced by observing its action in conjunction with other information; namely the market averages and the TICK indicator. We will look at these various applications in the balance of this chapter.

Figure 2–1 is a blank chart which can be very helpful in understanding the index and its changes throughout the day. It is suggested that the reader make some copies of this chart and use them on a daily basis for a few days. It will help him to develop an understanding of the way in which the index and the averages interact and the signals implied by various changes in the two. After a few days or weeks some will feel they wish to continue the practice, while others will rely upon their uncharted observations while using the knowledge they have gained.

The vertical dimension is plotted on a logarithmic scale and represents the values of the Arms Index. The log scale is used to compensate for the fact that bullish numbers can only be between zero and one, while bearish numbers can range upward from one to very large numbers. In this way there is more room to accurately plot the lower numbers, and the larger numbers are not likely to go off the page. The horizontal dimension is arithmetic and represents the plus and minus values of the change in the Dow Jones Industrial averages.

Figure 2–1

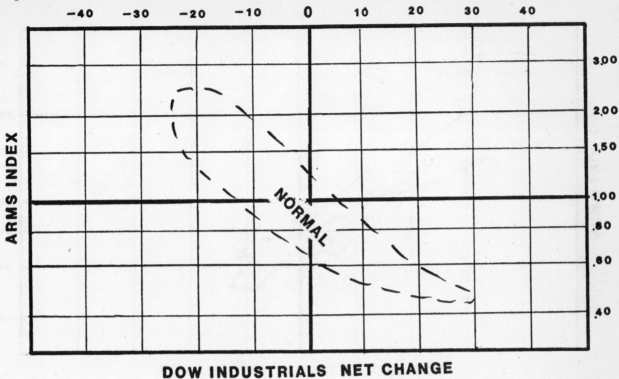

DOW INDUSTRIALS NET CHANGE

In using this chart, one starts with a new chart each day and enters a point shortly after the opening of the market. This point represents the value of the Arms Index based upon the vertical scale and the change in the Dow Industrials, plotted in reference to the horizontal scale.

Then, as the day progresses subsequent points are plotted and connected with arrows in the direction of time change. The points, we have found, should not be posted on a time basis such as every hour or every 15 minutes, but should be posted when a significant change seems to occur. Therefore, there will be times when a number of points may be posted in just a short time span while at other times no new postings may be made for hours if the market is doing nothing. It is not necessary to finish the day with an exact replication of the market, but rather with a chart that gives a fair idea of the types and magnitudes of the changes. The aim is not accuracy but knowledge. In fact, after the day is over you might just as well throw the chart away. It has served its purpose in keeping you aware of the market changes, and it will tell you little or nothing about what to expect in the future.

Figure 2–2 shows a recent, rather dramatic, trading day. The important turning points have been lettered in sequence as they occurred during the day. In response to a bearish overnight news item the market opened sharply lower. After the market had been open about 15 minutes, we plotted point A which represented an index of 2.78 and a Dow reading of minus 28 points. Due to the late openings of some stocks and additional weakness in others, the market moved lower until the market was down almost 50 points and the index was at 3.02; this is point B. Subsequent strength took the market to point C, with a further slight weakening

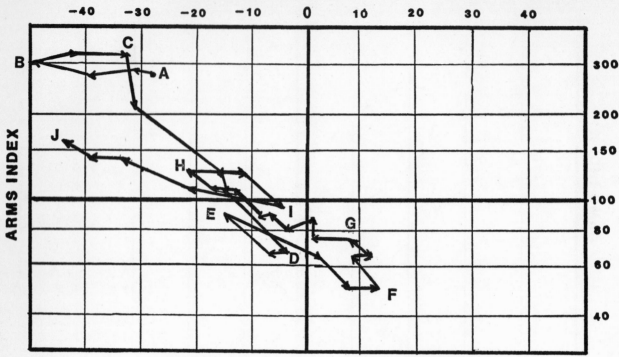

DOW INDUSTRIALS NET CHANGE

of the Arms Index. Then the market strengthened dramatically and the index moved downward in concert, so that point F was quickly reached, with one intervening detour between D and E where some selling was absorbed. At F the market had moved all the way into plus territory and the index was about .50. The move from F to G was significant in that the market retained its gains but the index had started to weaken. Herein was a warning that resistance to the advance was developing. Therefore, the decline from G to J was not a great surprise. Point J was the close of trading, with the market down about 45 points and the index at 1.65.

The two important moves on this plot were the vertical drop from C which represented a strengthening index prior to a strengthening market and the vertical rise from F to G which represented a weakening index prior to a weakening market. It can be seen, therefore, that the direction of movement of the index and its relationship to movement in the market can be very helpful in forecasting subsequent moves. Obviously, there will always be exceptions, but it is possible to formulate some generalities which hold true often enough to swing the odds in our favor. Usually an upward arrow will lead to market strength while a downward arrow will lead to market weakness. Horizontal arrows are signs of a move that lacks conviction; the market is moving but the index is not confirming the move. Moves from upper left to lower right represent normal strength which is likely to continue, and their opposite, moves from lower right to upper left, represent normal weakness which is likely to continue. The least common and least indicative moves are those along the angle from upper right to lower left and vise versa.

Figure 2–3 shows the significance of those moves. One should be aware that we are talking about direction of movement rather than about numerical values. These arrows can occur anywhere on the page with the same validity. There is, however, a separate interpretational value to the levels of the numbers themselves. It has been found that there is a normal range in which we would expect postings to occur. That is the area which we have outlined with dotted lines and marked as "normal" on Figure 2–1. Most postings will fall within, or very close to, that zone. When they do not, we know that we are dealing with unusual numbers. It has been observed that postings "prefer" to be within that zone, and movement of arrows shows a "preference" for the upper-left-to-lower-right orientation. Consequently, a point which lies well away from the normal zone is likely to be soon followed by a move which will place the next posting closer to the normal zone. Similarly, an arrow which is not in the upper-left-to-lower-right orientation is likely to be followed by an arrow or a series of arrows which swing the direction of movement toward this orientation.

Figure 2–4 depicts the various directions of arrows encountered and the probable next move which can be anticipated. The first arrow in each pair is the observed action, and the second is the anticipated result. There can be no

Figure 2–3

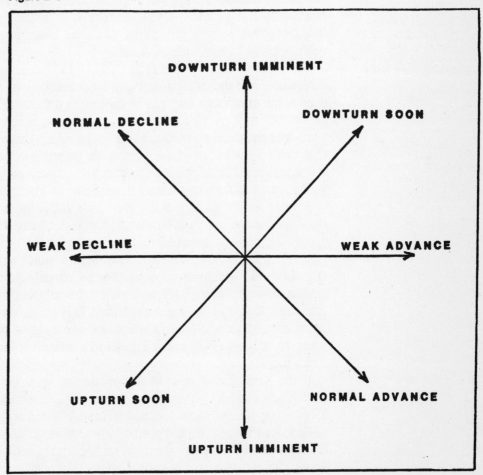

Figure 2–4

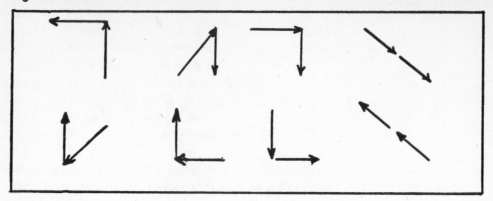

certainty that these will always work in just this manner, but the odds certainly favor the illustrated action.

We have spoken primarily, up until now, about the changes in the index. The actual numerical values are of consequence also. Just as in our longer-term studies, the index can become "too bullish" or "too bearish" at times. For example, a reading of .25 midway through the trading day would alert us that the buying was so concentrated in the advancing issues that it was not likely to be sustainable. Consequently, we might be inclined to hold off on buying until it returned to more normal levels. Similarly, a reading of 4.00 would make us suspicious that perhaps the selling had gone uncorrected for too long, and we might wish to buy into the weakness.

As with any observations such as those in the previous paragraph, there are exceptions, and the exceptions carry swift retribution. In very bullish markets, overbought conditions may persist far longer than seem reasonable; also, during periods of panic, oversold conditions may not correct for some time. In addition, there are sometimes anomalies in the index which are not immediately apparent. One or two stocks may have such huge volumes as to distort the index. The investor should, therefore, look for those distortions before acting upon a reading which seems to represent a very oversold or overbought condition.

A great additional help is the use of the TICK index. This index is merely a tabulation of the net ticks in the marketplace at any time. A stock whose last change in price was upward is said to have a plus tick, whereas a stock whose last price change was downward is said to have a minus tick. By subtracting minus ticks from plus ticks we get a number which may be positive or negative and represents the net ticks. This number is extremely sensitive to changes in market sentiment, leading even the Arms Index. It is so sensitive, however, as to carry erroneous signals and lead to whipsaws. We suggest that the aggressive trader watch the tick numbers and use them to confirm his judgement based upon the Arms Index.

If the Arms Index is used in conjunction with the changes in the market averages, it can be a big help in intraday trend recognition. The trader can use it to recognize turning points and take advantage of them; the long-term investor can use it to time his activity and position himself better. The intraday use of the index is only a small part of its value, but an important part. An interesting question is its significance on a closing basis. Can it tell us what to expect the next day? How about next week or next month? That is the subject of the next chapter.

Chapter 3 Closing Arms Indices as an Indicator

Does today's closing index give us some idea what tomorrow's market will be like? How about next week or next month? Are there tendencies which can make us money, or at least keep us from making costly mistakes? Let us take a look at the index in a number of ways, then, and try to answer these questions.

As in our previous work, our intent is the identification of trends which will help our timing. This means we are looking at the overall market, and then trying to relate that information to what action we might choose to take in the buying and selling of individual issues. This is not intended as a method of working with such instruments as market options. We are trying to swing the odds in our favor rather than to develop a "trading system," at this point. There are some applications, covered in other sections of this book, which are reliable enough to be treated as more of a system than a timing tool for those with the inclination and the fortitude to participate in such markets.

First, we plotted the closing index for each day and its subsequent day on an X-Y grid to see if there was some correlation between indices on a day to day basis. Each point in Figure 3–1 represents that plot. Today's index is located on the horizontal scale and tomorrow's is located on the vertical scale. This defines a location on the chart which has been plotted as a small rectangle. One hundred fifty days of information were plotted in order to have a reasonable-sized sample.

As would be expected, many of the plots fell near the intersection of the two 1.00 values. We assumed that these points would be of little meaning, only saying that most days were not very dramatic, and that most were likely to be followed by equally uninteresting days. What we were looking for, though, was the response to unusually bullish or bearish days. If a very bearish day was followed by another very bearish day, then the plot would fall in the upper-right-hand corner of the chart. Similarly, if extremely bullish days tended to be followed by other extremely bullish days, then the plot would fall in the lower-left-hand corner of the chart.

Looking at the chart, what we expected does not seem to be the case. There is a greater tendency for points to fall in the upper-left corner of the lower-right corner. This tells us, then, that there is a likelihood for a bearish reading on the index one day to be followed by a bullish reading on the index the next day, and vice versa. But wait, you say, there are quite a number of points in the lower-left area. This is certainly true, but one should be aware that the intersection of today's 1.00 and yesterday's 1.00 is quite far down in that corner, again due to the open-ended nature of the index toward high numbers. Even so, the tendency,

Figure 3–1

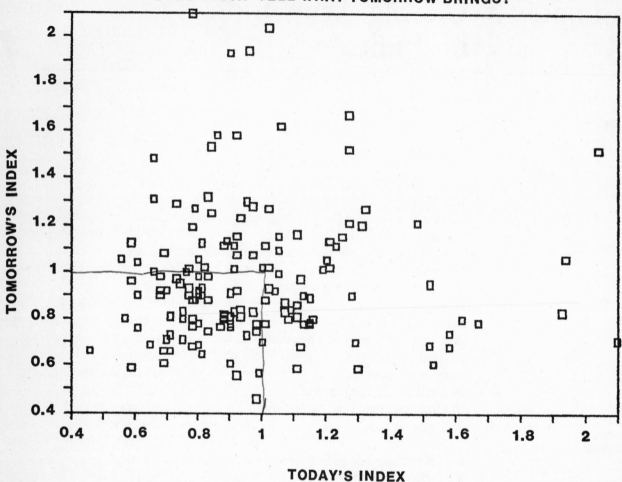

150 DAYS
DOES TODAY TELL WHAT TOMORROW BRINGS?

TODAY'S INDEX

although recognizable, seems rather weak. One would not, on this evidence, be
＊ a heavy buyer in the market because of an extremely bearish close, nor would one
want to sell stocks on the opening because the prior day was so bullish. Besides,
the index the next day does not necessarily mirror the market for that day. Often
a very bearish close on the index will be followed by a bullish index the next day
without the market responding equally well.

Perhaps it would be better to look at the market the next day rather than the
index the next day. After a very strong closing index, is the market more likely
continue up or to give back some of its gains? After a very high closing value for
the index, is the next day likely to further the decline or retrace some of it? To try
to find an answer to these questions we plotted each day's closing index by the net
change in the S&P 500 on the following day. The results of plotting over three
years of information is shown in Figure 3–2.

As in our prior example, we are looking for a response to unusual days. Most
of the data points fall, as would be expected, near the intersection of 1.00 for the
index and zero change for the S&P 500. Here we see clearly the tendency for the

Figure 3–2

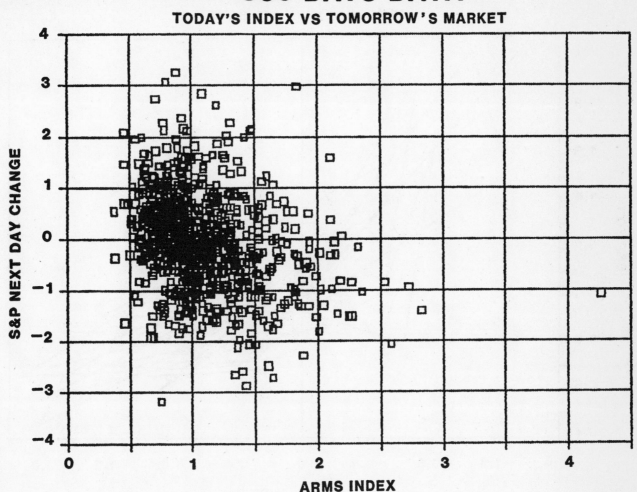

800 DAYS DATA
TODAY'S INDEX VS TOMORROW'S MARKET

more distant points to concentrate toward the lower-right and upper-left regions. This is telling us that a high-closing Arms Index is likely to lead to a strong market the next day, and a low-closing value is likely to portend a weaker market the next day. Evidently the market does have a tendency to become quite overbought or oversold, even on a day-to-day basis, leading to corrective action the next day.

Another look at the same concept is presented in Figure 3–3. The method of locating the points is the same as in 3–2 but now we have connected the postings with lines, so that the direction of movement is represented by the slope of the line. In order not to have too confusing a chart we only posted 50 points, but even with these the message is quite clear; the direction of motion is predominantly along the upper-left-to-lower-right trend. It tells us that the same tendency we saw in Chapter 2 for intraday changes in the market-to-index relationship is active in the day-to-day numbers. It reinforces our conclusion, reached from the prior example, that a weak market with a bearish index is likely to be followed the next day by a more bullish index and a stronger market.

Figure 3–3

50 DAYS
ARMS INDEX VS MKT SAME DAY

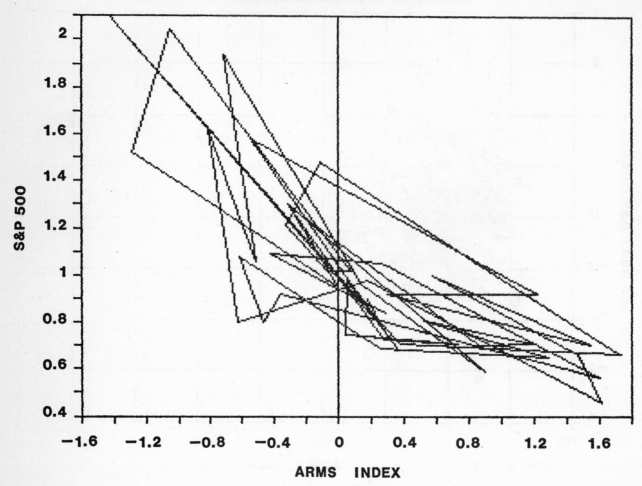

Is this a strong enough indication to use it as a market tool? We think it is a help, but not a deciding factor.

After a day in which the market closed very weakly on a very high index we would, on the following day, be watching closely for a turn to the upside, probably after some early follow-through of the weakness. We would be aware of the potential for a rapid change of direction, but would certainly not be buyers on the opening in anticipation of such a turn. Nor would we be immediate sellers just because the prior day had closed with an extremely low index. We would want to see more evidence and would go to our intraday studies for our timing. We would, however, be alert for a decline, since the prior day's close had warned us of it.

Perhaps, if the closing values of the Arms Index give us some idea of what to expect the next day, there is a similar longer term value. We explored this possibility using the same method as in Example 3–2 but extending the time frame. Figure 3–4 plots the closing index against the change in the S&P 500 over the next five days. Because of the longer time, the net changes are larger,

Figure 3–4

800 DAYS DATA
TODAY'S INDEX VS MKT MOVE 5 DAYS

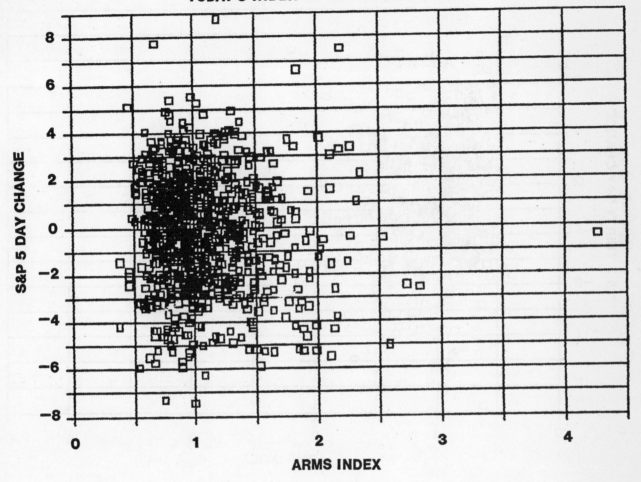

compressing the vertical axis to include larger numbers. Now, we see, there seems to be no recognizable signal. The concentration of points in the center of the data is normal, and the peripheral plots seem to be random. Evidently, as we go out a week, the significance of one day has diminished to the point where we can make no use of the information.

Just to be sure, we plotted the market change 30 days later against the closing daily values of the Arms Index. This plot, Figure 3–5, is, if anything, even more random. There is nothing here we can use.

We must reach the conclusion that the closing values of the index, used individually, lose their significance as we get further away from them. Evidently, if we are to have a worthwhile longer-term indicator, we will need to combine the information for a number of trading days.

Figure 3–5

800 DAYS DATA
TODAY'S INDEX VS MARKET MOVE 30 DAYS

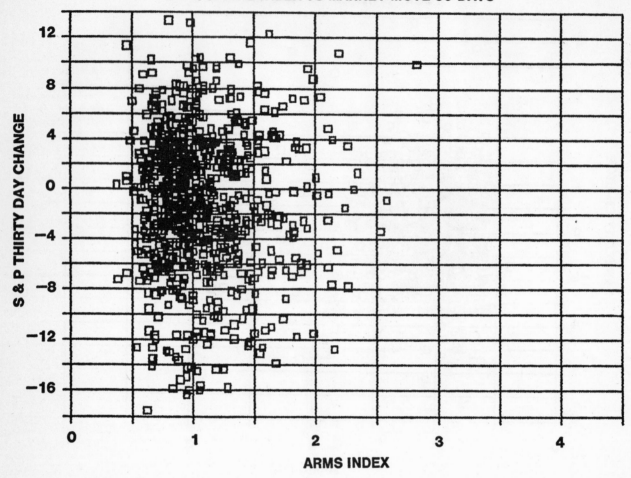

Chapter 4 Moving Averages

To this point we have talked only about the Arms Index as calculated from the advancing and declining issues and the advancing and declining volumes. It has become obvious, however, that we will need to massage those numbers, utilizing moving averages, weighting the components, and comparing results if we are to turn the index into a worthwhile longer-term tool. In addition, as will be seen later on, there are other exchanges besides the New York Stock Exchange to be considered. Therefore, we need to start this section by laying some ground rules as to terminology and abbreviations.

So far it has been easy. All we have looked at is the simple index and have merely called it the Arms Index. It will, however, get tedious for both the writer and the reader if we have to constantly repeat that name. So let us reserve that name Arms Index exclusively for the raw calculated value of the index and assign abbreviations to handle the many permutations and combinations.

In the prior three chapters, we have dealt only with numbers from the New York Stock Exchange since that has always been the basis of the index as used by Wall Street. There is no reason, however, for not making similar calculations for other exchanges, and we will be doing so in later chapters, arriving at some rather interesting results. So, let us agree to preface any set of abbreviations by a letter which indicates the exchange being depicted. Thus, the American Stock Exchange will carry the letter A; The Over-the-Counter market will be prefaced by an O, and the Bond index will be designated by the letter B. Another index, which we will introduce later and call the Giant Arms Index, will be identified by the letter G.

The second segment of our identification will always be the Arms Index, which will be abbreviated $A I$ except when used as its unaltered value. So, any calculation which involves the Arms Index as calculated for the New York Stock Exchange will start with the three letters NAI. The Giant Arms Index will start with GAI, etc.

The next letter, or set of letters, in our designation will indicate any unusual method of calculation. For example, if we are doing a weighted moving average there will be a W as the next letter. If we are doing an open moving average we will insert the letter O, etc. Each of these uses will be identified as we go along.

Finally, a number will show how many entries are being used in the calculation. For example, putting all of the abbreviations together, $AAIW21$ would be the nomenclature for a 21-day moving average of the American Stock Exchange Arms Index calculated as a weighted moving average. If we were studying a 30-day simple moving average of the Over-the-Counter Arms Index, we would name it *OAI30*.

Throughout the work that follows we will use a number of different moving averages of the index. The intent will be to zero in on the best indicators. The reader will notice, especially, the use of a number of rather unusual parameters. It has been customary over the years for technicians to use rather simple increments for their moving averages, usually 10 or multiples thereof such as 30, 100, or 200. The reason is simple. Before computers made such calculations extremely simple, the calculation of a moving average was tedious work. One had to add up the last "X" entries and divide by "X" over and over again. The chore could be made much easier if "X" was 10 or 100 since it eliminated one step. All that was necessary was to move the decimal point.

Unfortunately, the market was not aware of our mathematical limitations, and it did not feel the need to be tied to multiples of 10. Its natural rhythms were a result of supply and demand not of arithmetic convenience. In our explorations we have tried many different parameters; and having access to a computer, we felt no compunction to make its job easier by using less complicated mathematics. So we ran through many different moving averages in order to arrive at optimum results.

We have made a good deal of use of Fibonacci numbers in these studies. This series of numbers is constructed by adding the last two members of the sequence in order to arrive at the next member. The sequence, therefore, goes as follows: 1,2,3,5,8,13,21,34,55,89 etc. Three, for example, is the sum of the two preceding numbers, one and two; five is the sum of three and two, and eight is the sum of three and five. It is an endless sequence. The value of this sequence lies in our need to study a number of different parameters in order to find the most useful applications of the index. The Fibonacci sequence systematically stretches out the distance between numbers as we move out to higher numbers. This is valuable to us in that the exact value of a moving average becomes less critical to us as we look at longer time spans. Fibonacci numbers are not biased toward the decimal system, and they allow us to look at a number of divisors that are systematically spaced.

The Fibonacci sequence is often credited with mystical properties because of its uncanny recognition of numbers which seem to occur inordinately often in nature. In addition, these numbers seem to relate to various ancient ratios, particularly those used in the construction of the Egyptian pyramids. We will neither endorse nor refute these views, but merely use the sequence as a handy way of looking at a number of applications without being biased by the decimal system.

In dealing with very short-term moving averages, one step, as between 3 and 4, can make quite a difference, while the step between larger numbers can be quite inconsequential. For example, 21 is a favorite Fibonacci number to use with the Arms Index. Figure 4–1 shows our plot of that index for a six-month period in 1971. We then plotted the index for the same period, but used first a 20-day average and then a 22-day average. These are shown as Figures 4–2 and 4–3.

It can be easily seen that the shorter-term 20-day tends to have sharper spikes than the 21-day, and the 22-day has even more rounded turning points. This is to be expected. Longer-term moving averages are smoother. However, the three charts are so much alike as to impart the same information; the highs and lows and even the smaller jogs all coincide. It is hard to see how the 21-day average

Figure 4–1

SECOND HALF 1971
21 DAY ARMS INDEX

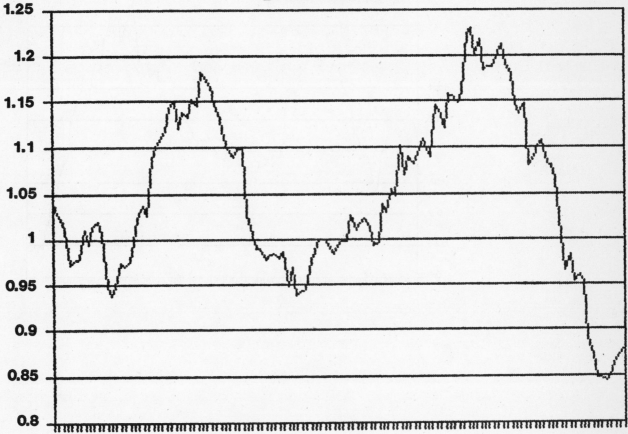

could be very much more helpful than the other two. But we will see, later, that a moving average of this approximate magnitude can be very valuable, be it exactly the Fibonacci number or one close to it.

In the chapters which follow, a large number of different examples have been used to illustrate certain points or examine certain applications. It should be made clear that the selection of particular time periods was not intended to be either random or biased, but illustrative. We have had the luxury of access to a large amount of data. Our files go back to 1968 when looking at the New York Stock Exchange figures, and even the data for the other exchanges goes back to 1984. Consequently, we have looked at a great deal more data than we have felt it necessary to include in the illustrations. The charts included are there because they illustrate the point we are trying to make, yet we have not included every time period for every point being made.

At times we have gone back to illustrations from 15 or more years ago, rather than using the most recent information. This is done in order to make it clear that the methods we are using are not reliant upon a recent phenomenon, but are usable in other markets at other times. The time lengths used in the illustrations also vary, dependent upon the point being made. If we are looking for a short-term trading help, we are likely to illustrate only a few months of trading

Figure 4–2

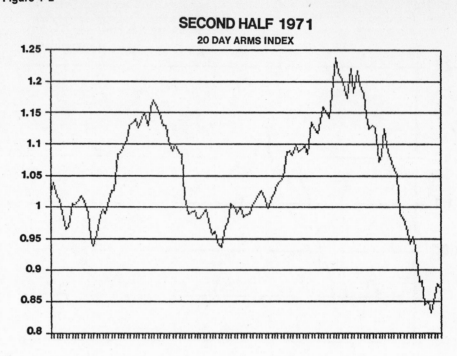

SECOND HALF 1971
20 DAY ARMS INDEX

Figure 4–3

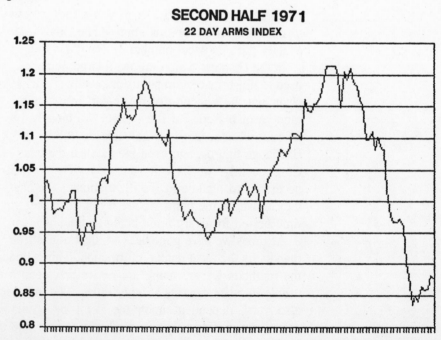

SECOND HALF 1971
22 DAY ARMS INDEX

history. This allows the closer scrutiny of each minor market swing. When looking for help in understanding long-term market swings, we include much longer time spans, usually many years, in order to recognize the important moves without being unduly influenced by the minor fluctuations.

It is tempting, when having so much data available, to pick out ideal examples to make a point. We have been careful to avoid this approach, and we have, in most cases, chosen examples that illustrate a point and show normal results rather than slanting the information toward ideal results. At times we will work with an approach in one time frame and feel that we have arrived at a strong correlation, only to find it far less effective when using it under different market conditions at another time. Whenever this happens we will point it out and look for a solution.

Chapter 5 Arithmetic Moving Averages—Short-Term

The most common and basic approach to the smoothing of data is the arithmetic moving average, or simple moving average. It entails merely averaging the data over a period of entries and continuing this process every time a new piece of data is added. For example, if we wanted to develop a three-day moving average of information from a series of days, we would add the last three entries and divide by three. Doing this each day, we would have a changing value; a moving average. The following data represents the calculation of a three-day moving average of the Arms Index during a recent market period.

Date	Arms Index	NAI3 (New York-Arms Index-3-day)
May 28	.70	
May 29	.62	
May 30	1.02	.78
June 2	1.13	.92
June 3	.87	1.01
June 4	1.07	1.02
June 5	.60	.85
June 6	.81	.83
June 9	1.57	.99

There is no value for the moving average shown for the first two days, since we need to accumulate data for three days in order to form a three-day average. On May 30, the value of the three-day moving average of the index is .78. This is arrived at by adding the last three values of the index, .70, .62 and 1.02, which comes to 2.34, and then dividing by three, for a result of .78. The next value is .92, which represents the sum of .62, 1.02 and 1.13 divided by three.

Any time one works with a moving average, he is compromising in order to smooth data. The smoothing is done by including past data with current data, which means letting today's immediate and important information be diluted by yesterday's or last week's less important information. It comes to a toss-up between a long-term moving average which is smoother and more easily understood and interpreted on the one hand, and a short-term moving average which is more sensitive and responsive while containing wild gyrations and whipsaws, on the other hand. Of course, the length of the moving average is also somewhat decided by the intentions of the investor. If he is a short-term speculator he will be looking for smaller moves which develop quickly, and will, therefore, need to use a very responsive moving average. A long-term investor may not need to watch each fluctuation and will be better informed by a longer-term moving average. We will look at a number of applications, keeping these factors in mind.

Let us look at the shortest-term moving averages first and move outward from there. A moving average is, of course, more sensitive to small changes when we are looking at a short-term application, so we will look at every possibility as we study the shortest-term moving averages. As we move outward to longer-term averages we will start to skip some numbers. As we saw in the last chapter, there is little difference between a 20, 21, or 22-day moving average of the same data.

In the third chapter, dealing with intraday uses of the index, we saw that the daily closing numbers seem to have little predictive value except as related to the day immediately following. It was evident that there is a tendency for a very bullish day to be followed by a bearish day, and a very bearish day to be followed by a very bullish day. One day with a very high Arms Index reading does not seem to reliably tell us anything about the market a few days or weeks down the road.

Our first moving average is a two-day calculation. This is shown in Figure 5–1, and it depicts one year of trading. Above the index is shown the action of the Standard and Poor's 500 stock index for the same period. We have used 1986 for our example and will follow through with other indices for the same year, in order to be able to compare the effectiveness of various time frames. Surprisingly, in view of the uninformative nature of the one-day figures, the two-day figures are dramatically closely related to subsequent market action. One needs only to look at the peaks on the index to realize how closely they correlate with low points in the market. If we run a line across the first illustration at the 1.60 level of the NAI2, we see that there are six occasions during the year where the NAI2 moved to values above that level. We have labeled them A through F on the market chart. Similarly, we arbitrarily chose the .60 level as the overbought parameter and observed the incidences of penetration of that level. There were five, which have been labeled M through Q on the market chart.

It is interesting that the daily figures seemed so random, yet the two-day figures were so positive. We observed that in most cases a bearish day is followed by a bullish day and vice versa. Those days would cancel each other out on a two-day moving average, and give no signal. The strong signals come in when that tendency is blatantly violated. Evidently, strong emotional responses in the marketplace can be expected to last one day without carrying a great deal of longer-term significance, whereas buying or selling frenzies that carry over for two or more days represent a trend and imply an emotionalism which will need to be corrected in the near future.

We must keep in mind the fact that we are looking for changes of direction in the market; changes which are brought about by oversold or overbought conditions. Our signals to buy are produced, not by other people buying, but by other people selling. We are looking for situations where an emotion, be it fear or greed, has run for too long. This puts us into the contrarian camp. We want to trade against the crowd, recognizing those times when the public has let fear prevail over reason and has sold stocks indiscriminately. This is our chance to buy. Similarly, when the public has been preponderantly on the buy side, pushing prices up without giving the market a breather, they push the Arms Index into very

Figure 5–1

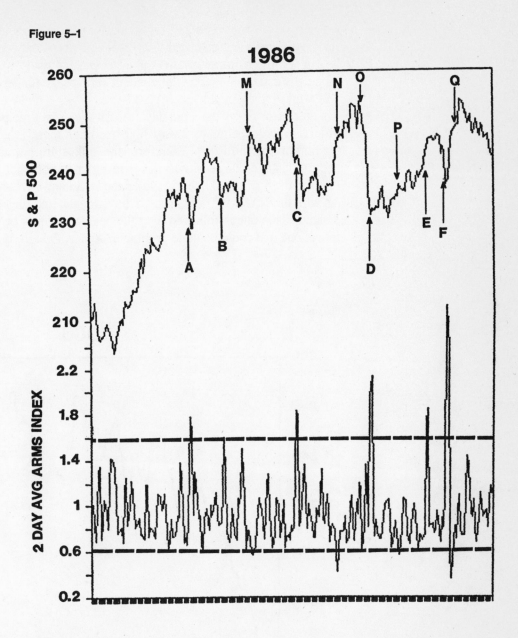

low numbers and indicate an overbought situation. If they are that anxious to own stocks at any price, we should be willing to satisfy their greed, by selling them stock.

Looking more closely at the two-day AI we see that the buy signals are all very good, but somewhat early. This implies that it takes at least two days to start a trend, but once established, that trend has further to go. On the other side of the market, with the sell signals which we lettered *M* through *Q*, there is also a tendency to be a couple of days early, but it does not appear as critical as the buys. We could deal with this in one of two ways; we could wait a few days after each signal in order to let the move run its course, or we could try to move out to a longer-term moving average which would give us a more coincident signal. The problem with the first alternative is our own emotional involvement in the market. It is very difficult to see a market that looks very oversold and yet sit back and wait before buying. The day following two very oversold days will usually be stronger, convincing us that the reversal is upon us and we are about to miss the boat. For those who can handle it, the "signal and wait" method can be effective, especially in trading market options, but perhaps the longer-term moving averages will work; let's take a look.

Figure 5–2 shows the three-day NAI for the same time period as before. As we observed above, after two very high readings there is a tendency for a lower reading on the third day. Therefore, the spikes are not as pronounced, and we need to change our sensitivity level in order to see enough usable signals. We reduced the buy signal line to 1.40 on the NAI3 and have shown that on the chart. As with the NAI2, we now have six buy signals, and they appear to be very well located. Each one is followed over the next two weeks or so by a strong upward move; one that could be quite profitable. Again, though, the signals are a little bit

Figure 5–2

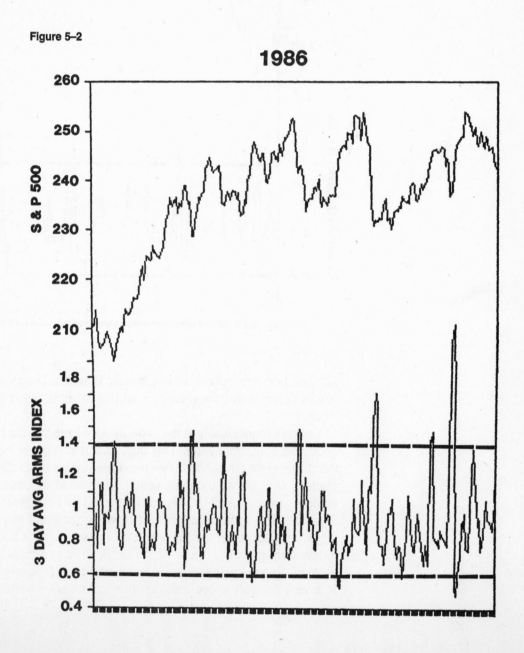

1986

early. Acting on them would lead to profits, but waiting a day or two would usually enhance those profits.

On the sell side, we found there was no need to change from the .60 level as an indicator. Now, instead of five sell points we have four, but the one that was eliminated was one of the best. Also, there seems to be a continuing problem with getting the signal too early. Our conclusion, then, is that the three-day is only marginally better than the two-day on the buy side, and it shows no improvement on the sell side. Let us, therefore, move on.

The four-day AI is shown in Figure 5–3. As with the three-day, we have had to lower the signal line on the buy side, now to 1.30, and have also been able to raise the sell line to the .70 level. The result has been a retention of the same six buys, but now at a better time and with the addition of one sell, but at an earlier date, one we had not seen before. The NAI4 seems to be accomplishing what we were searching for. It catches the buys at or near the optimum level, it does not

Figure 5–3

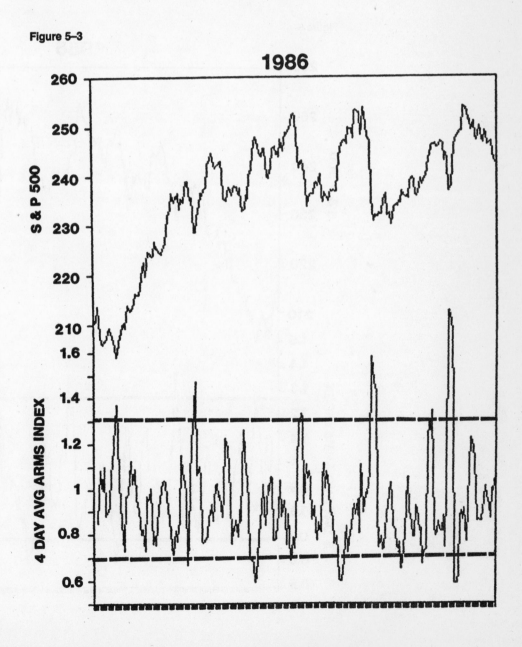

seem to give bad signals, and the sells seem to be well placed and effective. A very important additional point, something we did not see in the earlier examples, is the alternative buy and sell signals. Each buy is followed by a subsequent sell at a higher level, allowing one to trade "signal to signal." The exception is the occurrence of two consecutive buys late in the year. They would have both been profitable with the sell which is the last signal on the page, however.

Moving on to the five-day AI in Figure 5–4, we have again moved the buy parameter, this time to 1.25. This seems to have an unexpected result. Instead of bringing the signal in later, it tends to take us back to our previous problem of signals that came in too early! Perhaps there is a tendency for some preliminary high numbers before the signal producing two days of heavy selling. We feel, therefore, that the five-day is less helpful than the four-day in making short-term buy decisions.

Figure 5–4

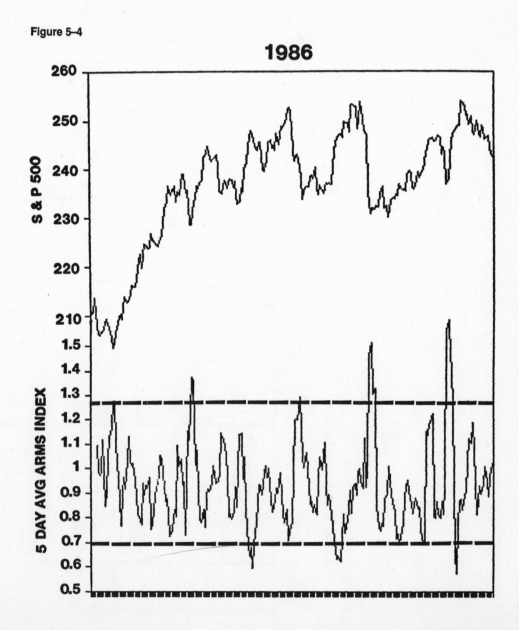

On the sell side, the five-day parameter was kept at .70. To make it more sensitive by going to .75 or .80 would have triggered a much larger number of sell signals, but signals which would not be helpful. Staying at .70 cut us back to only three sells, thus eliminating the ability to trade "signal to signal." It appears, then, that the five-day is not as good as the four-day. Perhaps we have exceeded the optimum level for short-term trading. Let us look, however, at a longer-term average and see.

We will skip each intermediate step, now, and try an eight-day moving average (Figure 5–5). The logical buy parameter on this chart seems to be 1.15. As with the five-day, the interesting tendency to give short-term signals too early is quite noticeable. To try to avoid this by moving the buy level up to 1.20 would eliminate the first buy signal of the year, which turned out to be the most profitable. We could, instead, move the level to 1.25 and eliminate all except two signals, which would be quite profitable. Now, however, we are getting into the

Figure 5–5

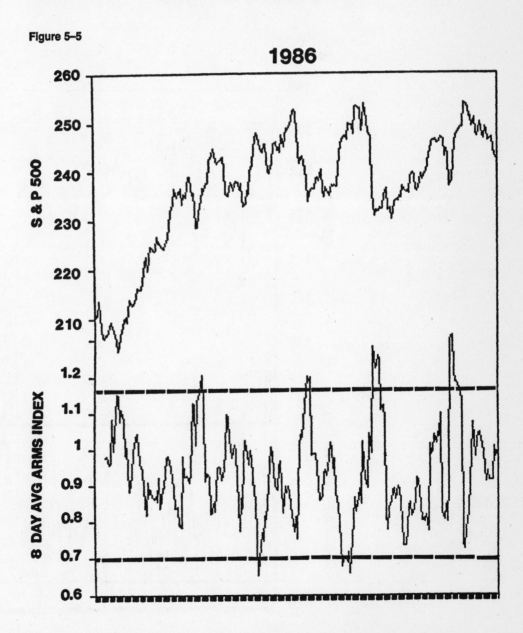

recognition of fewer but larger moves. This will be addressed better by looking at other averages of longer duration. That will be the subject of the next chapter.

On the sell side, we have the same problem as we were faced with in the five-day parameter. A sensitive level will pull in many useless signals while a less sensitive level will give us too few signals. The .70 level seems to continue to be the best, but it is not really as satisfactory as we would like.

Based on this one year of history, we have found that the four-day moving average of the Arms Index and the parameters of 1.30 and .70 seem to yield the best results for the aggressive market participant. One year is not enough evidence, however. Let us look at other cases.

Figure 5–6 shows the market for the year 1981, as measured by the S&P 500, and below it is shown the NAI4 for the same period. As with 1986, we have drawn in the 1.30 and .70 levels. Again, we have six buy signals, but now they seem to be coming in early, especially at point C. On the sell side there are only two points, but they are quite good.

Figure 5–6

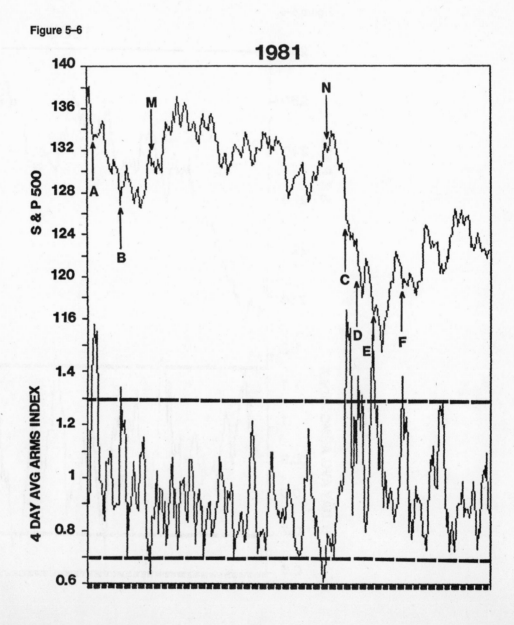

It appears that our rules which worked so well in 1986 were not as effective in 1981. The reason is, perhaps, a difference in the longer-term nature of the market. The year 1986 was a part of a five-year bull market. There was an upward bias to prices, and a bias toward low numbers on the Arms Index. On the other hand, 1981 was a poor year in the marketplace. Prices were trending downward and the Arms Index was showing more high readings. Therefore, we are seeing a bias toward higher numbers, thereby producing buy signals too soon and not producing enough sell signals.

Perhaps what is needed is an adjustment for overall market conditions. We will explore that option in a later chapter as we start to combine indices. In the meantime, however, we have an index which, although not perfect, does provide us with some very good short-term trading opportunities.

Chapter 6 Intermediate-Term Arithmetic Averages

A standard analogy used by technical analysts over the years has been one which compares the action of the market to the ocean. There is a progressive series of disturbances of the water, from tiny ripples to tsunamis, and a similar series of superimposed waves in the stock market. When related to the stock market, each of these market moves can be used to generate profits if used correctly, and if misunderstood can lead to losses.

The water surface is continually disturbed by ripples just as there is a constant rhythmic fluctuation in the underlying stock prices which thereby create a similar ripple effect in the overall market. So far we have been looking at the ripples which last only a few hours or a few days. We have seen how they can help us to maximize profits by entering or leaving the market with our individual issues at propitious times. We also have been able to put a few days' data together and develop indicators which can be helpful in actually trading, especially if one is using a market proxy such as an option on a group of stocks.

These ripples are, however, superimposed upon a wave pattern. The waves, at any time, have a fairly constant amplitude and wavelength. As we stand upon a beach and watch the waves crash on the sand, we have to be aware of the distant powerful storms which must have poured their energy upon the ocean to cause such a disturbance. As market observers we know that there are strong fundamental forces which are heaping the waters of the stock market into waves. As technicians, we are not concerned with the nature of those storms, but rather with their effect. As with the sea, we know that a nearby storm will produce a more confused surface, with cross patterns in the waves, and high steep waves which often interfere with one another or reinforce one another. Distant storms cause the regular rhythmic rollers which are the metronome of the sea.

Standing on the beach, we are less aware of the larger pattern of the ocean, the tides. Yet, this is an even more reliable and regular rhythm of the water, predictable centuries in advance. The market has similar longer-term fluctuations which are not obvious to the shorter-term observer. These are the major trends, the bull and bear markets.

In the last chapter we attempted to recognize and profit from the ripples. These moves, often lasting just a few days, were best identified by using short-term moving averages of the Arms Index. We found, however, that we soon reached a point where the longer-term moving averages tended to fail us, masking rather than revealing the peaks and troughs of the ripples. After we got beyond a four-day moving average our results seemed to be less satisfactory. This is to be expected. It is much like the problem faced by physicists in trying to study subatomic particles. The target is smaller than the photons which might be used to observe them.

However, light is not too big to study molecules. Perhaps we can move up to a larger target, and our longer-term indices will be able to shed some meaningful light on the subject. The logical target is the next step up in our sea analogy, the waves. These market moves, which last a number of weeks or months, are quite regular as to amplitude and wavelength, and they provide an area of profits for those who are not inclined to be traders, yet do not want to just participate in the longer-term tidal moves, the bull and bear markets.

In studying the validity of longer-term indices we have started to look at longer time frames in our charts. In order to locate helpful parameters, we have chosen a three-year period, 1978, 1979, and 1980. During this time the market had two years of sideways action, followed by one year with a good advance. More importantly, however, the market went through a number of fairly large swings; moves large enough to make it fairly likely that the investor would be able to make money by being on the right side of the market, even if his individual stock choices were not stellar. Figure 6–1 shows that three-year period, as measured by the S&P 500 stock index.

Before looking at indicators, let us decide what periods we would have liked to have recognized. We have labeled the chart with the letters *A* through *H*. These are turning points which seem to be significant enough to serve our purposes. There is a pullback between A and B which is tempting, but is really too small for our purposes. Also, there are a number of swings between C and D which are interesting, but again too small, so our choice of the points shown is somewhat arbitrary. What we are looking for are moves which represent a minimum of a 10 percent profit. Some of these moves represent a much larger profit than that.

What we have identified, then, is a series of four long positions, interrupted by three periods of either being short or merely out of the market. Since we are

Figure 6–1

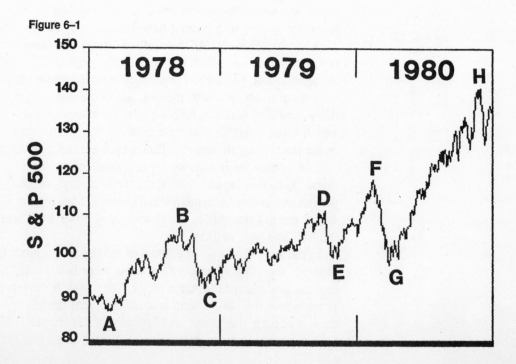

looking at three years of history, that means that we are encountering an opportunity to make money on the long side of the market a little more than once a year. What is needed, therefore, is an indicator which will identify those opportunities as soon as possible, yet one which will not give erroneous signals.

The attempt to recognize the turning points in the wave pattern using the Arms Index has been approached in many ways by many analysts. In using arithmetic averages, the most common use has been the 10-day moving average. As we pointed out before, this is a natural outgrowth of our decimal system, and it was adopted to suit the convenience of the analysts rather than the rhythm of the market. It speaks well for the underlying validity of the index that it was so successful while having the constraints of convenience imposed upon it. The 10-day moving average is very widely followed, and numerous advisors key much of their forecasting to this computation. It does, in fact, serve very well to recognize overbought and oversold markets. The problems with the NAI10 are that it tends to find the points too soon and it finds too many if we lower our response level to a point where it will find the points we wish to locate, especially on the sell side.

Figure 6–2 shows the plot of the NAI10, as compared to the market. We have chosen to put our signal-generating lines at .70 and 1.20, in order to recognize the

Figure 6–2

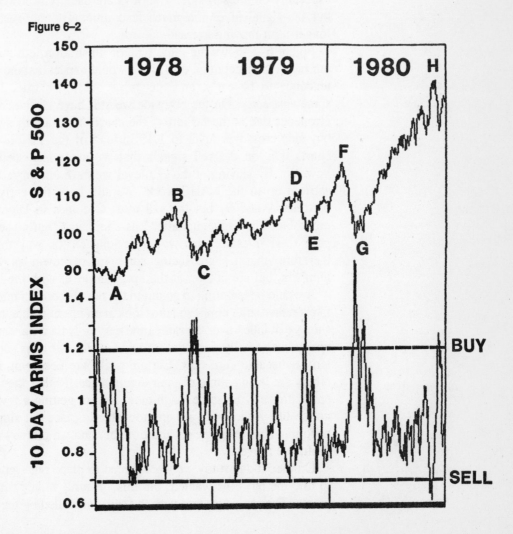

best buys and sells. Note that all of the desired buy points show up but they seem to be early. The move above 1.20 very early in 1978 eventually led to a good market advance, but the move did not start for number of weeks, and started from a somewhat lower level. The only way to recognize the sell point at B was to put our sell level at .70, but this then dragged in an earlier sell which was not followed by a rebuy; the upshot being that we would sell too soon and miss a good deal of the move. Had one ignored the first sell, the second sell, which corresponded to point B, was a little early but was certainly effective in light of the drop that began shortly thereafter.

The buy area at point C was emphatically signalled, albeit too early. The market moved upward after the signal, but, unfortunately, a sell signal was again generated before the move was over, and at such a time that there would probably have been little or no profit. The second sell signal in this sequence came in a little before the top at D, setting the stage for a reasonable profit on the short side between D and E. Then, between the very good buy at E and the top at F, we got a disastrous sell signal which took us out before the move got going. The buy at G and the sell at H were both excellent. Finally, at the end of 1980 we got one more buy signal. Looking on to 1981, we see that it would not have been a profitable long position, since the market went sharply lower.

We would conclude, then, that the NAI10 leaves room for improvement, especially on the sell side. The buys are usually followed by a market advance, but the signal gives too much lead time. This suggests that we should try a longer-term moving average.

Figure 6–3 shows the same type of illustration, but this time we have gone to our next Fibonacci number; 13. We would expect that the signals would show less tendency to be early, and this turns out to be true. However, they still are somewhat early. On the buy side we still have all the same buys, including the erroneous one at the far left of the chart. To attain these results we lowered the buy-side crossover level to 1.15 instead of the 1.20 level used for the NAI10 chart. It is on the sell signals that we are really seeing some improvement, however. By staying at the .70 level we have eliminated two of the sells which showed up in the NAI10 work. We still have the early (but profitable) signal between A and B, but the sell after C comes in later, and is therefore more profitable. The bad signal after E is eliminated, but no sell signal at all comes in prior to H, meaning one would be long all the way from E to H. It appears, therefore, that we are seeing some improvement as we move out to larger numbers, but are not yet at the optimum level with the NAI13.

It would be tempting to go out to the next Fibonacci number, 21, but that seems like a rather large jump, so let us look at an intermediate value, say 17. Figure 6–4 shows that index over the same time period. Now we are starting to see a tendency which has actually persisted throughout these studies, but has not been particularly noticeable until now. Certain peaks are becoming more pronounced while others are losing some of their significance. Rather than having many spikes of approximately the same magnitude, we are getting a few which are much more noticeable. As a result, we are now able to place our signal levels in such a way as to intercept fewer peaks and troughs, and we thereby identify fewer but more profitable moves.

On the 10-day study we were forced to place our signal level at 1.20 in order to find the buys we wanted, but this, in turn, brought in some undesirable buy points. The same was true with the sells, signalled by the .70 level. We ended up

Figure 6–3

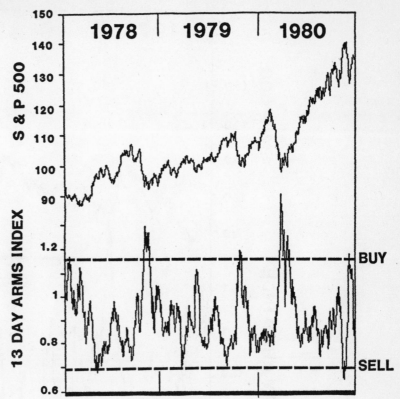

Figure 6–4

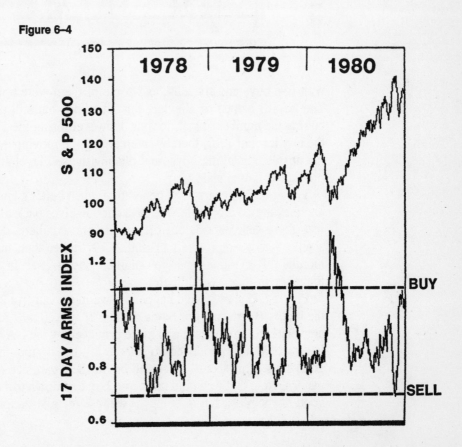

44

Figure 6–5

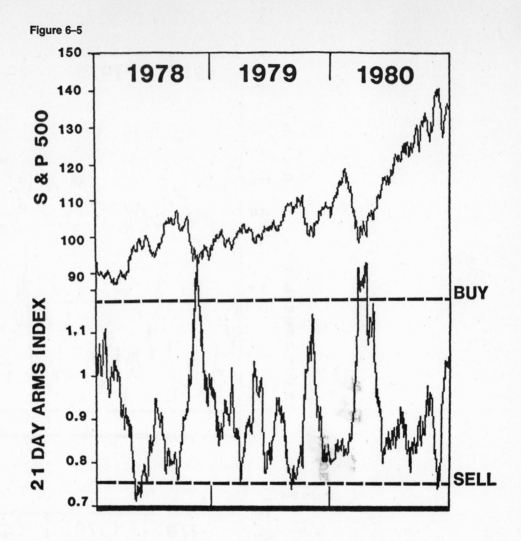

with five buys and six sells, and some of them were not really what we wanted. The NAI13 helped to alleviate this situation, but still produced five buys while cutting the number of sells to four. However, using the 17-day index we can place the buy level at 1.10, thereby intercepting the moving average line three times on the upside, signalling buys, and placing the sell level at .70 again, but now only producing two signals.

The NAI17 appears to be generating much better signals! They are very timely, and they are all profitable. We have cut ourselves back to only three long positions in a three-year period, but the results are excellent. However, it does seem a shame that we didn't sell in mid 1979, rather than holding through about six months of gyrations before another buy signal in early 1980. Perhaps a longer-term index would help.

Figure 6–5 shows what happens if we move out to a 21-day moving average of the index. By placing our buy signal level at 1.20, we generate buy signals which are very similar in location to those produced by the NAI17. Using .70 for our sell level would have produced no sells at all, but by moving up to .65 we see three good sells. This seems, so far, to be our best parameter for identifying the wave pattern. Note that we could move our buy line down to 1.10 and bring back in two good buy signals, but in doing so we lose the alternation of buy and sell signals.

Figure 6–6

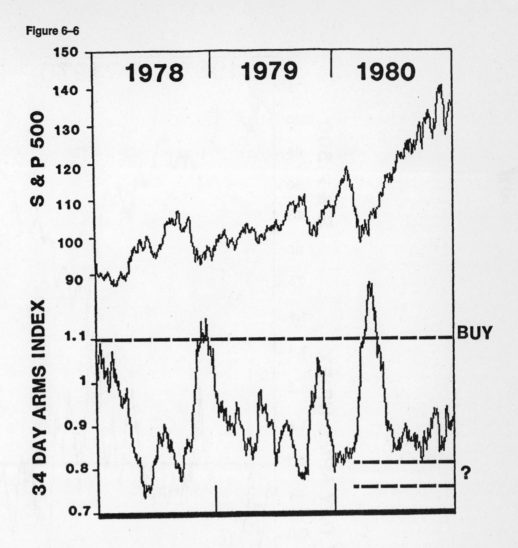

It seems better to keep the wider parameters and to trade fewer but more reliable waves, and waves of larger amplitude.

Looking at the NAI34 in Figure 6–6, we seem to have little improvement on the buy side. The same buy points are defined if we use the 1.10 level for our signals, but they are a trifle late. On the sell side, .75 gives too few signals, and .80 gives too many. It appears we have gone past the best level of computation. Either the NAI17 or the NAI21 seem to point out the opportunities quite well.

Is this three-year period enough evidence? Perhaps it is too simple. Let us take a look at another period and see if it still works. Figure 6–7 represents the same type of study, but almost a decade earlier. Here we are again looking at a 17-day moving average of the index and comparing it to the S&P 500. By running our signal levels at the same values as used before, 1.10 and .70, we get an entirely different picture. We end up with eight buy points and no sell points. Of course, every buy point is soon followed by a significant market advance, so that the signals are valid and certainly continue to exhibit the reliability of the index. The problem arises from the fact that there are no sell points.

The difference in results is a function of the underlying market tone. In much of the 1969-through-1971 period, the market was in a sharp decline, and in the

Figure 6–7

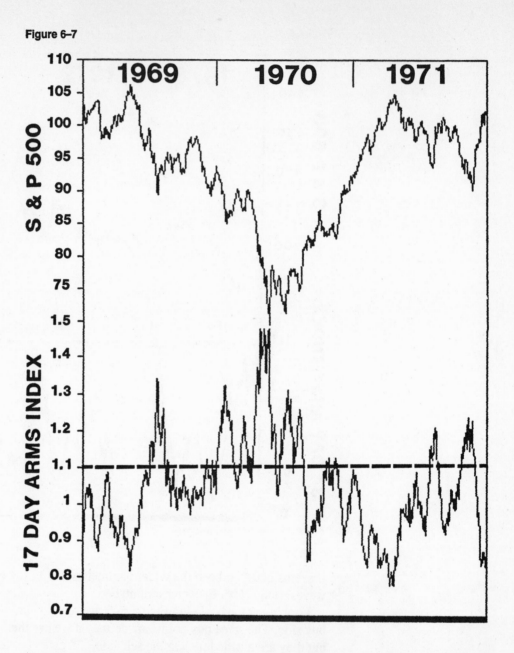

balance of the period there was a strong advance. In the 1978-through-1980 period it was more of a sideways market. In a sideways market, horizontal lines as signal levels were satisfactory, but in a market with strong trends the index seemed to stay too bullish in one part of the chart and too bearish in another. It would seem that we need to adjust the crossover levels for the nature of the market.

This is exactly the problem we ran into on a shorter-term basis in the prior chapter. If we want indicators which identify the extremes of a wave pattern, we need to understand and recognize the larger wave pattern which is effecting it.

Chapter 7 Combining Indices

Let us suppose we are standing at the end of a dock built out into the bay. Looking over the side down at the water, we see that there is a wooden horizontal brace which is just above the water level, and another which is just a short distance under water. It is a breezy day, and waves are rolling in toward shore. We notice that most waves do not come up high enough to touch the upper bar, but occasionally a larger wave comes along which does barely lap against it. Similarly, most wave troughs do not expose the lower bar, but from time to time a particularly deep trough will show us the lower crosspiece. Aha! We are now convinced that we have established the normal levels of waves and that we can recognize significant extremes when they touch the crossbar on the upside or expose the crossbar on the downside. We go home content that we have discovered a reliable indicator.

Later that day, just to be sure, we go back down to the dock and take another look, and we are dismayed to see that the crossbars are completely immersed, with even the deepest wave trough unable to expose the upper bar. When we looked before it was low tide; now it is high tide.

Being unusually intrigued by this phenomenon, and desiring a better wave-amplitude indicator, we invent a simple device. Instead of having the crossbars fixed to the dock, and thereby subject to the variations of the tide, we attach the two crossbars on a float which can go up and down with the tide. As before, one is above the water and the other is under the water. Now we can watch the wave pattern and recognize the extremes of amplitude without worrying about the stage of the tide. Of course, the float itself will tend to rise and fall somewhat with the waves, but since it is so much larger than the waves, the movement will be unimportant in our observations.

Our problems in the prior two chapters are quite similar to the above analogy, and the solution is also similar. We have found that the next larger wave pattern is throwing off the accuracy of our signal levels. We have tried to nail the crossbars to the dock and have ignored the tidal fluctuations.

Let us consider first the longer-term work from Chapter 6. We had decided that the 21-day Arms Index was giving us very reliable signals, but that the signal levels changed, depending upon the nature of the underlying market. However, it was obvious, even in the last example, that the peaks and troughs of the 21-day index coincided extremely well with optimum buy and sell points in the market. Since the 21-day worked so well, we will retain it and try to introduce another factor, which will vary the level of the signal line depending upon the nature of the underlying larger wave pattern.

In Figure 7–1 we have looked again at the 1969-through-1971 period which was giving us problems at the end of the last chapter. Now, in addition to the NAI21, we have inserted another, longer-term, moving average. We have gone out to the NAI55, which should smooth the information for us. Using a single line in this fashion is like placing one indicator bar on our float a short distance under water. In this illustration we will then want to be in the market when the faster line, the NAI21, is below the slower, NAI55. We will want to be out of the market, or short, when the NAI21 is above the NAI55. When the faster index is high, remember, it is bearish, and when it is above the NAI55, it is more bearish than the norm for that market.

Figure 7–1

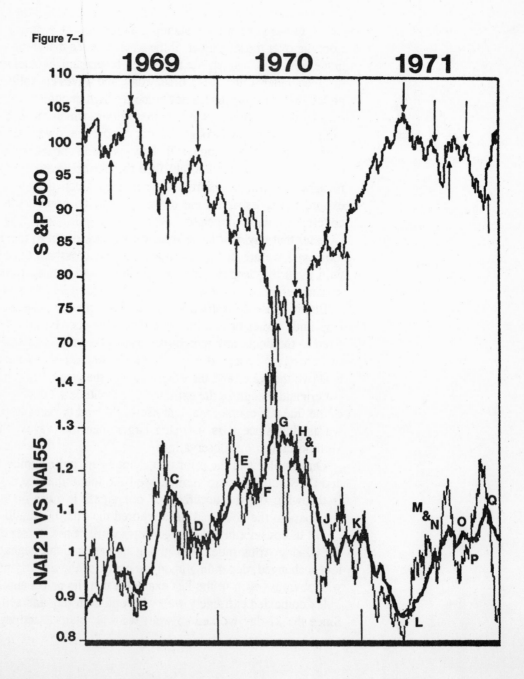

We have lettered each crossing point on the chart and then transferred these points to the upper part of the chart which represents the market over the same time period. We have assumed that we would buy stocks when the NAI21 dropped below the NAI55 and cover the position or go short when the indices crossed back the other way. The results are astonishing! Every long position is followed by a substantial upward move, and every short position is similarly effective. One should be aware, however, that the crossovers are sometimes hard to read, and the signals are sometimes either early or late. There are two very quick moves which might have been hard to use. There are at H-I and M-N.

This method has one decided advantage. It always alternates buys and sells, thereby protecting one against overstaying a bad position when it does occur. The greatest danger in using this method, we state from experience, is ignoring a signal and hoping it will soon cross back the other way. A discipline which is as accurate as this one seems to be is not to be second-guessed by intuition.

It should be noted that we have tested a large number of indices before arriving at the 21–55 combination. This seems to be the most useful for intercepting each wave. The 21–89 combination, for example, gives almost exactly the same signals, but does not seem to be as timely. Following the 21–55 combination over many years, we find it has continued to be reliable. Since it is compensating for the level of the tide it gauges the waves very well.

If there is a drawback, it is the frequency of trades. We have found ourselves back in the world of traders rather than investors. As a result, we are moving on smaller fluctuations, ones which may not be reflected in the individual stocks we are trading. We can easily be right on the market and still not make money on the stocks we have chosen to own.

When we were just looking at fixed buy-and-sell levels in the prior two chapters, we assumed that there was a neutral zone between buy levels and sell levels, whereas in this work a sell signal or a buy signal is generated by the same line, the NAI55. Could we get better results by removing the single indicator from our float and replacing it with a pair of indicators, one below water level and one above? Perhaps it would make our signals more accurate, and it might get rid of the smaller waves.

To achieve the desired results we calculated the NAI55 and then multiplied that result, first by 1.10 to create a value representing 110 percent of the NAI55. Next, we calculated another series of values which represented 90 percent of the NAI55. We then plotted these two lines over the NAI21. In this manner we defined a "normal" range for the NAI21 and could observe those points where the NAI21 moved outside of the range. The result is shown in Figure 7–2.

The results are nowhere near as good as using the single-line indicator. The reason is simple; we are forced to wait too long before acting, making our actions late. We had hoped to eliminate some of the trades by acting only on extremes, but instead found that we were making almost as many trades, but they were not as effective. It appears that our best way of recognizing good trades on an intermediate-term basis is the crossovers of the 21-day and 55-day moving averages of the Arms Index.

We have found before, however, that conclusions reached by studying a particular time period did not hold true when we moved to another example, so let us look at another time period. In Figure 7–3 we see the same overlapping of the 21-day and the 55-day indices, but now for 1978 through 1980. Again, we have a large number of buy-and-sell points; nine of each. We must remember,

Figure 7–2

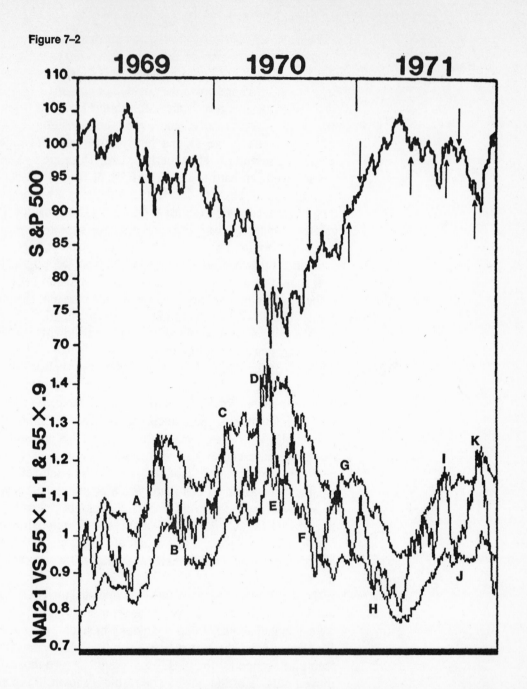

however, that this is a three-year period, so we are averaging three long positions and three short positions per year. In other words, we would hold our average position for two months. This is not long-term investing, but neither is it short-term trading. We are trying to take advantage of the wave pattern rather than either the ripples or the tides.

As before, the results are very good. Every buy leads to a higher sell. If we also were to have used the short side of the market, we would not have done quite as well, but, nevertheless, the results would have been good. Because this method calls for alternating buy-and-sell signals, one is not wrong for long. The next signal, if obeyed, keeps one from overstaying a bad position.

We seem, with this approach, to have found a very effective way of identifying the intermediate pattern. The answer lay with overlapping arithmetic moving

Figure 7–3

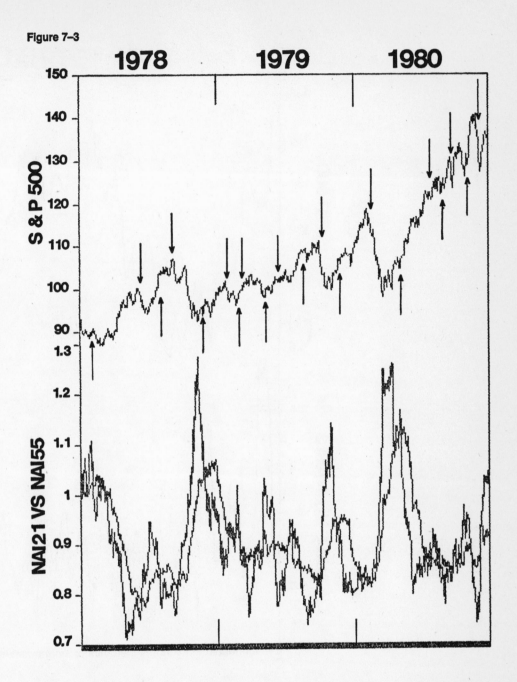

averages. Maybe the same approach would work with the smaller wave patterns also. In Chapter 5 we were trying to identify the buy-and-sell points in the ripple pattern and found that the four-day moving average seemed the most effective. We were not completely satisfied, however. As with the longer-term work, our results were not reliable when we went to another time period in which different market conditions prevailed. Perhaps we could achieve better results using the same approach, but on a shorter-term basis.

After experimenting with a number of different longer-term indices, it became apparent that the 13-day moving average, when used in conjunction with the 4-day average, gave a number of crossovers which were fairly well in tune with the market. Figure 7–4 shows that pair of indices and their relationship to the market during the first six months of 1981. Notice that we have shortened the time

Figure 7–4

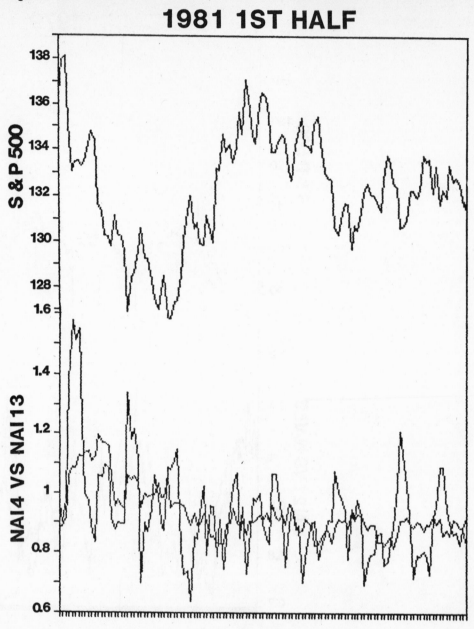

1981 1ST HALF

span. It was fine to look at three years of history when we were searching for a few good trades per year, but when dealing with the ripples, it is necessary to stretch out the time scale in order to see what we are doing. Even so, the picture is far from clear. There are so many crossovers one quickly gets lost trying to interpret the chart. To get around the problem we made an additional calculation, wherein we asked the computer to subtract the value of the NAI13 from the value of the NAI4, and plot the results as a bar chart (Figure 7–5). Now, the crossovers are much easier to see and relate to the market.

If similar signals have the same meaning as they did in the longer-term work, then we should look for buys whenever the bars move from the downside to the upside, and we should expect sells whenever the bars move from the upside to the

Figure 7-5

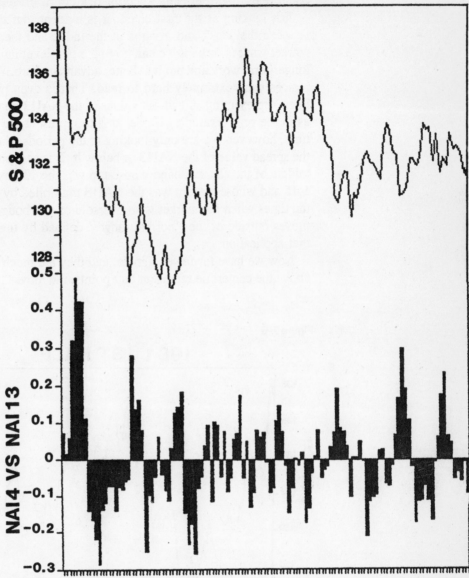

1981 1ST HALF

downside. In other words, we would be long during the entire period when the bars are above the centerline, and we'd be short during the time the bars are below the centerline.

The first few positions seem to be quite effective, but after that there are a number of bad signals which could have been expensive. Then, in the middle part of the chart, there are many very short-term crossovers which would have done little more than generate commissions for the brokers. We appear to have developed too sensitive of an indicator, one that tends to be early. In just six months it gave eighteen buy signals and eighteen sell signals. That comes out to an average holding time of about three and a half trading days per investment. Of course, none of us would object to that many trades if they were profitable, but that does not turn out to be the case. Perhaps enough of the trades would make money so that the method would be satisfactory, but there does seem to be a close correlation between the index and the market, which could be better used if we could find a more effective way of reading it.

Just looking at the first chart, it is evident that there is a strong correlation between the peaks and troughs in the index and the high and low points in the market waves. Perhaps we can go to the two-level indicator which we tried in the longer-term work and put it to better advantage here. We found before that the two indices were extremely hard to read. That is even more true when we put two lines, representing spread-out values of the NAI13 on top of the NAI4. Therefore, as in the prior example, we decided to represent the NAI4 on a bar chart. This time, however, we are only looking at the periods when the NAI4 is either above the spread value of the NAI13 or below it. It is as though we cut a band out of the middle of the chart; a band whose top was the 13-day Arms Index multiplied by 1.15 and whose bottom was the NAI13 multiplied by .85. The bars are depicting the times when the market is so oversold or overbought that the short-term index moves outside of the "normal range" defined by the NAI13. Figure 7–6 shows that application.

Now we have far fewer signals, and they are much more effective. The moves above the centerline represent buy points; the moves below the centerline are sell

Figure 7–6

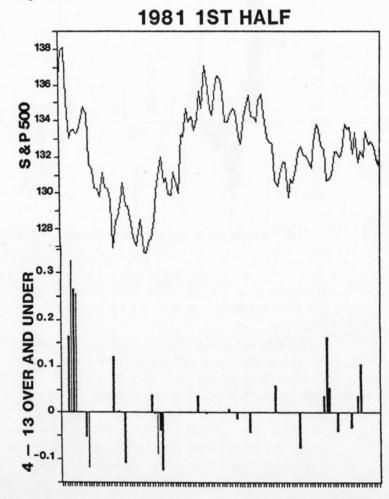

1981 1ST HALF

points. We have eight buys during the same six-month period, rather than eighteen, and every one is soon followed by a substantial market advance. On the sell side there are now only eight signals, also, and all are effective. There are two instances where a sell signal is followed by another sell without an intervening buy. This is what happens when we use a band of values rather than a line. The increased accuracy more than compensates for this drawback, however.

We have tried this graphic method over a great number of time spans, and we have found it to be extremely accurate in locating the very short-term turning points in the market. In Figure 7–7 we have depicted a different six-month period in the same way. One can easily see how useful this method would have been.

Have we now revealed to the readers a floodlit path to incredible riches? Is this a foolproof indicator? Sorry, but we don't think so. Not that it isn't accurate, but we must remember that knowing the market and knowing individual stocks are not the same. The shorter the time span studied, the less likely it is that an individual issue will act in concert with the market. As a timing tool, however, the above short-term method will usually help to buy and sell at the right time.

Of course, market options can be used as a proxy for the market, and a very nimble trader should find this tool extremely useful. The pitfalls are the same

Figure 7–7

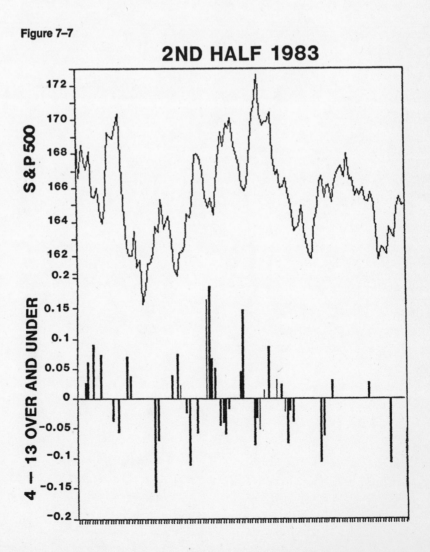

pitfalls as accompany any option trade; options are highly leveraged, so that one wrong move can wipe out all of the gains from a number of good decisions. In addition, as a wasting asset, options may be effected by other factors besides the underlying market; namely time and the public's apprehension as time runs short on an option.

We have now looked at, and arrived at, satisfactory methods for forecasting moves in the market, both short-term and intermediate-term. In the next chapter we will look at the usefulness of the Arms Index in the recognition of much larger moves.

Chapter 8 Tides and Tsunamis

We have seen in prior chapters that this simple index, if viewed in the right way, can act as a predictive tool for the market, both short-term and intermediate-term. The market, however, is influenced by much longer-term cycles. These are the great bull and bear moves which take years to develop and run their course. We need to see if those moves can also be recognized and capitalized upon.

In addition, occasionally but not often, a deep rumbling earthquake so shakes the bedrock of our economy that a great upheaval spreads devastation through the financial markets. The resulting tidal waves, or tsunamis, can spell the ruin of years of construction. Fortunes can be swept away in minutes as the powerful wave crashes down. We need to see if the index can warn us of such impending disasters.

Over the last 20 years we have kept detailed daily records of the Arms Index, calculated in a number of ways, and posted in conjunction with various market averages. Looking back over this market history, there have been just a few major market bottoms, preceding very large market advances. The first occurred in mid 1970, and it was followed by an advance lasting about three years and moving prices upward on the average stock by about 100 percent. The next was in late 1974, and it was an extremely significant market low. From there the market advanced quite steadily for six years, again showing a doubling before its next decline. After moving downward from late 1980, another important low was made in the summer of 1982. It was from this level that the major bull market started, which lasted until the third quarter of 1987; over five years. Of course, each of these moves was interrupted many times along the way, but the interruptions, in retrospect, appear to be pullbacks within the larger structure described above.

We have calculated and plotted the Arms Index over those 20 years, using two longer-term values which seem effective; the 55-day moving average and the 89-day moving average. Figure 8–1 shows the first 15 of those years. The upper line depicts the action of the stock market during that time, while the lower plot is actually two lines superimposed. These are the 55-day and the 89-day moving average lines. It can be seen that one line is more volatile and has sharper peaks and troughs, while the other is more rounded and tends to have a less amplitude. This less responsive line is the NAI89.

The two highest points ever reached by the NAI55 (prior to the 1987 panic, which we will look at later) were: a little over 1.30 in 1970, and 1.34 in 1974. They coincided very closely with the market bottom in each case. There were two

58

Figure 8-1

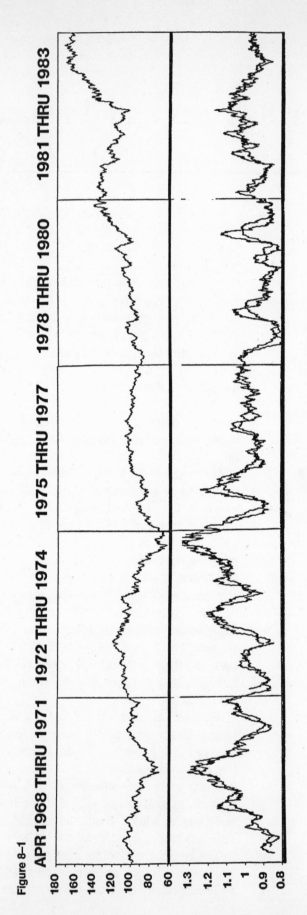

S & P 500 vs NAI55 & NAI89

other instances when the NAI55 was in the 1.20 area, and, although both were at low points which could have led to profits, neither could be construed as major tidal lows. One was in 1973, the other in 1975. The next highest peak during this 15-year period occurred precisely on the bottom of the market in 1982, marking the beginning of the greatest bull market since the 1920s. The NAI55 was just below 1.20. The market low in 1984, which was a resting point in the bull market, did not carry such a high reading in the index. In fact, the NAI55 stayed at more bullish levels throughout the entire bull move.

It would seem, then, that we should watch the NAI55 if we wish to take advantage of the very large long-term market moves. Any value of 1.30 or higher would seem to be signalling a very low-risk buy point. Even somewhat lower values should be interpreted as areas of opportunity. So, in the oversold direction, at least, we now have an indicator which tells us when we can take long-term market positions. Of course, it can be argued that two really good buy signals and one quite good buy signal are not enough evidence upon which to base a decision. However, the fact that the index is also so effective in shorter-term studies, where more evidence is available, would tend to add to the credibility of the long-term work.

Wondering if the 55-day was not long-term enough, we also ran the same studies over the same time period using an 89-day moving average. Interestingly, the values at the peaks and troughs for the NAI89 were just a few hundredths away from the value of the NAI55, but the same exact message was imparted in every case. The NAI89 tended to be a little late, however, causing one to leave a little money on the table. Our conclusion: stick with the NAI55.

So far, we have talked about the buy signals only. What about the sell side? We found that the lows in the index, which should coincide with the tops in the market, did very much as we hoped. The problem was a glut of signals. Yes, the index went below .90 whenever a major market top was made, but it also did so on intermediate-term tops. It is as though there are many degrees of oversold, but only one degree of overbought. Our interpretation, or perhaps rationalization, is the belief that fear is a far stronger emotion than greed and that panicky conditions can create extremely bearish indicators, whereas avarice tends to plateau, bringing about similar plateaus in the index.

The fact that we get a great number of sell signals does not invalidate the significance of the NAI55 for determining tops. It should be judiciously followed. Remember, it is going to point out the major tops as well as the intermediate tops, so any signal should be regarded as a warning. A long-term investor might not choose to sell all his stocks on a sell signal, but a lightening up or some profit taking would certainly be in order.

There is one additional clue, however. Most of the moves to low numbers were spikes, with the index touching .85 or even .80 and then quickly moving back toward a more normal reading. However, in the more significant market tops the index stayed in overbought territory for a longer time; a period of months. Perhaps a sell signal is more important if it stays in effect for a longer period.

Let us now look at the most significant market top since 1929; the 1987 period which marked the end of the bull market which began in 1982. This was one of the devastating tidal waves we mentioned at the beginning of the chapter. Our problem is the lack of other similar panics which can be studied. The last one prior to 1987 was in 1929, and we have no data to cover that period. Therefore, we have but one example to guide us. Let us see, however, if we can identify

60

Figure 8–2

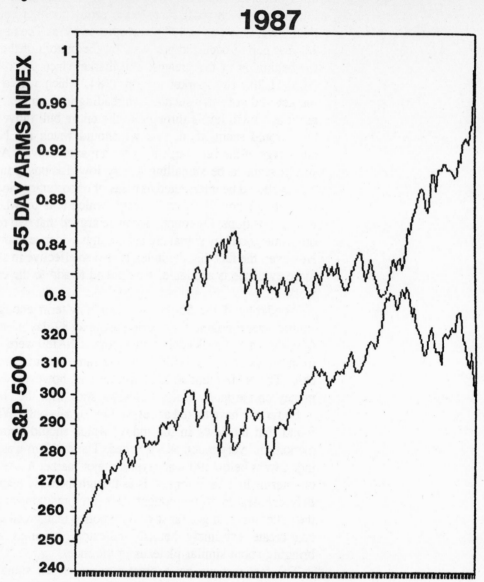

anything unusual. Figure 8–2 shows the NAI55 and the S&P 500 for the year 1987, but only until October 16. We did not show the rest of the year because the unusual action of the crash would make our charts much harder to read.

What appears most significant here is the fact that the index not only went down below .80, but it stayed in that neighborhood for a long period of time. It certainly was saying that the market was extremely overbought. Whether this signal will be valid at some future date when the market again tumbles is hard to say. However, the fact that it was the most overbought indication we had seen in the last 20 years, and that it led to the most dramatic market break in the last 20 years, has to be considered. Any investor seeing the same conditions a few years from now would be well advised to do some selling, just in case.

Chapter 9　The Open Arms Index

It has become popular among financial letter writers and other analysts over the years to make changes in the computation of the index in hopes of improving upon results. Most of these variations have started with the index computed in the traditional manner and then applied mathematical techniques to that series of numbers. We will be looking at a number of these techniques in a future chapter. However, one technique which has become very popular goes further back and changes the method of computing the daily index. This has become known as the "open" calculation.

According to Peter Eliades, publisher of the newsletter *Stockmarket Cycles,* and the most widely known user of the "open" variation of the index, the open calculation was first suggested by Harvey D. Wilbur in 1983. Largely as a result of Mr. Eliades' work, the open calculation has gathered a large following.

In calculating the index in this way, a moving average is constructed of each component of the index, and the index is then calculated from the results of each moving average. Table 9–1 shows the calculation of an open 10-day average and compares it to the standard calculation as explained at the beginning of the book. The first four columns are the components used to calculate the index; advances, declines, advancing volume, and declining volume. These are daily numbers for the New York Stock Exchange; hence, the headings are preceeded by an N. The fifth column is the index calculated in the normal manner. So that we will be able to compare the results, we have next calculated a 10-day moving average of the standard Arms Index.

Column 7 is the first part of the calculation of the open index. This number which we have labeled "10 ADV" is arrived at by constructing a 10-day moving average of the advances shown in column 1. Similarly, the next three columns are the 10-day moving averages of columns 2, 3, and 4, respectively. The last step in the construction of the open 10-day index is to plug in the standard formula, but this time to the 10-day moving averages rather than the raw numbers. This results in the 10-day Open Arms Index, shown in the last column. The calculation is shown below for the first value.

$$\frac{\dfrac{A}{D}}{\dfrac{AV}{DV}} = \frac{\dfrac{801.6}{777.1}}{\dfrac{5696.7}{4810.2}} = \frac{1.032}{1.184} = .87$$

Table 9-1

NADV	NDEC	NAVL	NDVL	NAI	NAI10	10 ADV	10 DEC	10 AV	10 DV	NAID10
1093	559	10184	3631	0.70						
896	694	6392	3881	0.78						
608	1013	2469	6869	1.67						
792	713	4838	4784	1.10						
1198	401	11516	1618	0.42						
800	820	5520	6804	1.20						
681	877	3978	5594	1.09						
651	900	3514	4358	0.90						
809	759	5607	4490	0.85						
488	1035	2949	6073	0.97	0.97	801.6	777.1	5696.7	4810.2	0.87
581	996	2733	5262	1.12	1.01	750.4	820.8	4951.6	4973.3	0.92
480	1101	2792	5048	0.79	1.01	708.8	861.5	4591.6	5090.0	0.91
997	549	7664	2528	0.60	0.90	747.7	815.1	5111.1	4655.9	0.84
740	812	4482	5039	1.02	0.90	742.5	825.0	5075.5	4681.4	0.83
800	672	5177	3381	0.78	0.93	702.7	852.1	4441.6	4857.7	0.90
1109	471	10140	2380	0.55	0.87	733.6	817.2	4903.6	4415.3	0.81
561	964	3265	5723	1.02	0.86	721.6	825.9	4832.3	4428.2	0.80
703	807	4725	5309	0.98	0.87	726.8	816.6	4953.4	4523.3	0.81
561	972	3285	7014	1.23	0.91	702.0	837.9	4721.2	4775.7	0.85

This calculation is done repeatedly, arriving at a value for each day. For the person doing the calculations by hand, the calculation of this index is a much more burdensome chore, although with the aid of computers the problems are quickly eliminated. In keeping a number of different open indices, the work becomes even more burdensome, since each change of parameters adds four more moving averages to calculate, rather than just one.

If we look at the results of the two calculations, the open and the standard calculation, as shown in the sixth column and in the last column, we see that they are behaving very similarly; when one goes up the other goes up. However, even with this small sample it is apparent that the open calculation gives consistently lower readings. Let us look at a larger number of data points and see if this is still true. Figure 9–1 compares the NAI10 and the NAIO10 during the first six months of 1984. The heavier line is the NAIO10; the open calculation. There is no time in the entire six months when the standard calculation is appreciably lower than the open calculation. In studying many years of history, this has been found to be invariably the case.

The reason for this difference is based upon the fact that the standard calculation of the index produces numbers which can be infinitely large, but not infinitely small. A bearish reading (over 1.00) can be any value from 1.00 to

Figure 9–1

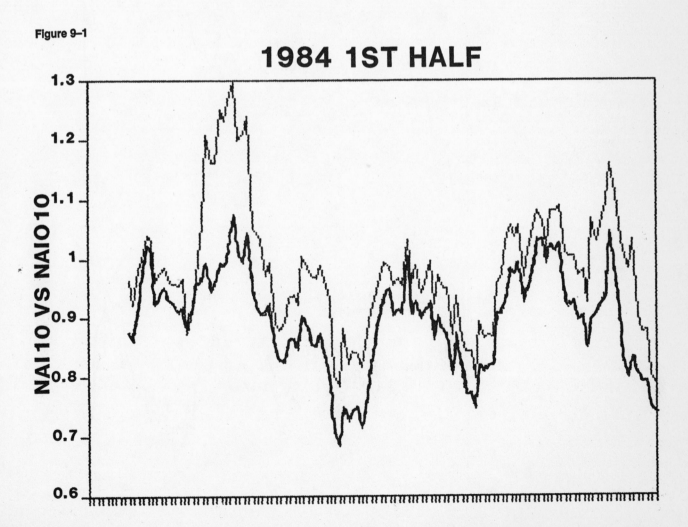

1984 1ST HALF

infinity, whereas a bullish reading (under 1.00) is restricted to a value between 1.00 and 0. This generates a situation in which the larger numbers are having more influence on the moving average than the smaller numbers, thereby causing somewhat higher values for the standard calculation than for the open calculation.

Mathematicians and other purists are often bothered by this, whereas pragmatists only want to see if the different calculation is more effective. The open calculation is one way of eliminating the bias toward larger numbers. Another is the use of the semilogarithmic charts.

Since most analysts who use the open index seem to concentrate on the 10-day, let us look at the NAI10, compared to the NAI010 and evaluate the results. Figure 9–2 shows that comparison for the first half of 1985 and plots both indices below the S&P 500 market average for the same period. As before, the heavier line is the

Figure 9–2

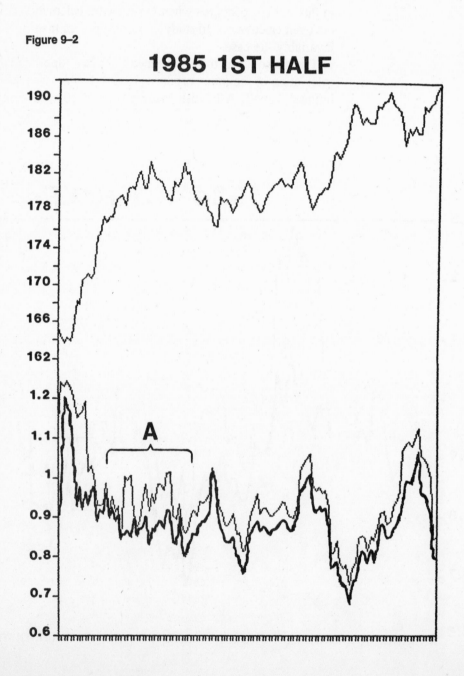

1985 1ST HALF

open index. The first difference which comes to light is the sharper peaks in the open index. This tends to be true for all periods studied. The normal calculation which creates an oversold market has a more lingering effect. The index tends to be saying "buy" for a longer period of time. In the open index the signal is sharper, with the index then quickly returning to a more neutral reading. Champions of the open calculation point this out as an advantage, arguing that the buys are pinpointed and unequivocal. We agree with this finding and consider it an advantage, but are somewhat bothered by the fact that the same effect tends to make most peaks in the open index of more nearly the same amplitude. This results in a uniformity of signals for most oversold markets, whereas the standard calculation tends to see more difference between oversold, very oversold, and very, very oversold. This difference often is a clue to the magnitude of the subsequent rise.

The most striking factor in these comparative charts is the parallelism of the two lines. It appears that either line will do a very good job of locating markets which have seen too much selling for too long and are ready to turn up. It is unimportant that one gives lower readings than the other. We are only interested in relative levels. In the bracketed area marked *A* the open index remained neutral, whereas the standard index found some minor, but profitable, buy points. Otherwise, the buy areas match well, both in timeliness and in recognizability.

Looking at the low points on the chart, the sell points in our interpretation, either method seems to do equally well. Neither method appears to be superior. We have, however, seen some historical examples where overbought conditions produced a more dramatic spike in the open index. This can often be helpful, since tops are always much more difficult to identify than bottoms when using the index.

As we said, the 10-day is the most popular use of the open index. In prior chapters we have seen that the standard calculation is more helpful if we use parameters other than the 10-day, so let us look at the open index in other ways also. First, we will compare the 4-day with the open 4-day. Figure 9–3 shows both the open and the standard calculation plotted together for the year 1986. Here, it is apparent that the two indices are almost identical. Only on the peaks is there any variation, and this is in magnitude rather than direction. The higher points are a result of the standard calculation. Throughout the chart the two lines are almost exactly the same, and certainly the signals are the same. We must conclude that the open calculation does not help us in any way in better recognizing the ripple pattern of the market.

The next really strong parameter in the standard calculation was the 21-day moving average. In Figure 9–4 we have plotted the two different calculations of the 21-day index, again for the year 1986. Here, it is even more apparent than in the 10-day work that the values for the open index are consistently lower. The open index is the heavier line on this chart. In general, the two indices are imparting the same information to the analyst. However, there are a few discrepancies. There are five good buy areas, lettered *A* through *E*, which are well recognized by the standard index. Point E, however, is missed by the open calculation. On the other hand, point B is more accurate on the open index. Looking over large volumes of history we have concluded that there are always a few discrepancies between the two methods and that neither method is necessarily better. It is still obvious, however, that the 21-day calculation is one of our strongest parameters.

Figure 9–3

1986

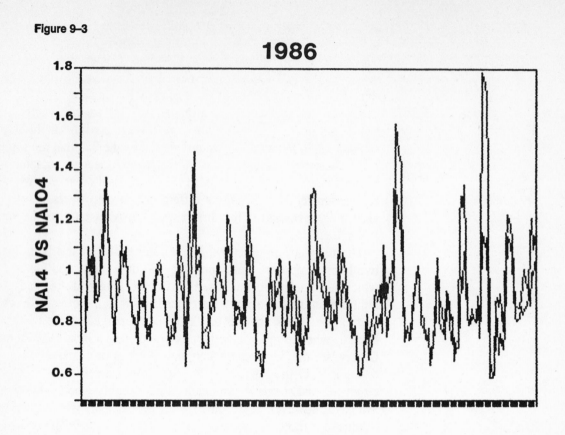

Figure 9–4

1986

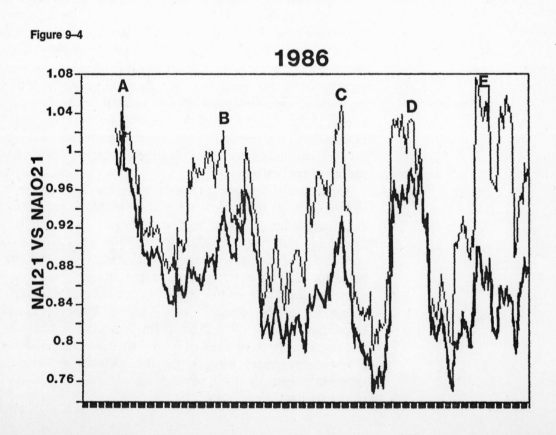

Figure 9–5

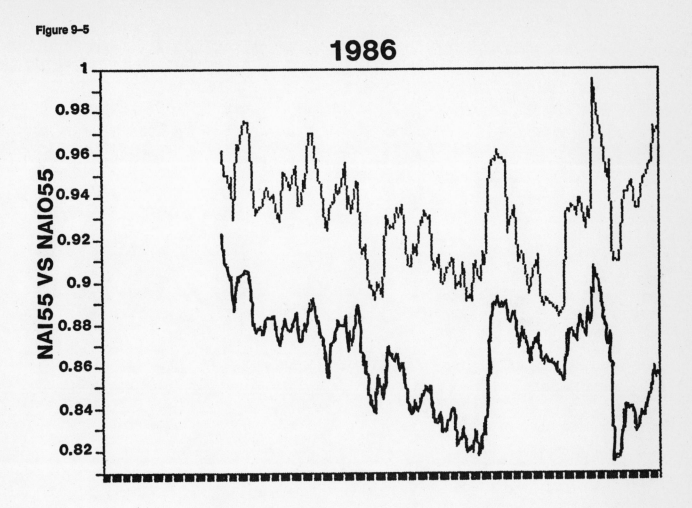

1986

Moving out to the 55-day calculations we find that the lines are even more parallel. We have plotted these in Figure 9–5, with the open calculation as before, the heavier line. Again, the lines sometimes are giving slightly different readings, but we fail to find a consistent advantage in one method.

In view of the fact that there seemed to be some differences between open numbers and standard calculations, we wondered if any advantage could be gained if we duplicated the prior work of crossovers between two moving averages using the open indices instead. A great deal of time was spent on this work, using both long-term and short-term indices, yet no worthwhile improvement could be discerned. We continue, therefore, to favor the parameters and indices used in Chapters 7 and 8.

Chapter 10   Predicting the Bond Market

The Arms Index was, of course, devised as a method of studying the stock market, and as we have seen, it is very useful in this regard. Logically, however, there should be nothing to limit the index to equity markets. The index is evaluating a supply-and-demand picture, and it should be useful in any supply-and-demand market. More specifically, however, the index can only be used if a free, double-auction market exists, and it can only actually be calculated if price and volume figures are available for that market. For example, there is an active market in works of art, but there is no centralized reporting system of either prices or volume of trading, so no index can be calculated. If, however, the figures were available, it is logical to suppose that an "Art Arms Index" would be helpful in recognizing when Rembrandts or van Goghs had been run up or down too far.

Certainly some such measure could be very helpful in the real estate market if statistics were available. This is a very similar market to the stock market, but trading is not centralized, and neither prices nor volume of trading are reported. It would be logical to assume, however, that heavy trading of house lots, with ever-increasing prices, would eventually lead to an overbought market. Perhaps by knowing the number of lots trading at higher prices and the number of lots trading at lower prices we could, just as with stocks, know when the move was overdone.

One other market is centralized, however, and has long beckoned us as a place to apply these methods; the bond market. Here we have an organized reporting system in which price movements and volume of trading are made public. Until recently, however, one would have had to do a great amount of calculation to arrive at these figures. The number of advances and declines have been reported for many years, but there has been no source for the advancing and declining volume figures, the other part of the formula. One could, of course, add up the numbers in the newspaper if one really wanted to make the calculation.

We are grateful to John Bollinger CFA, who is the technical analyst for the Financial News Network, for leading the way in this work. It is his data we will be using in this chapter. As a proxy for the bond market, we will be using the price of CBT Treasury bond futures for the closest month. The numbers for advancing and declining issues and advancing and declining volume are composite numbers. The source for these numbers is not easy to find, but John gets them from Hale Systems Inc., 2 Seaview Blvd., Port Washington, N.Y. He then makes his calculation of the Bond Arms Index and includes the results in graphic form in his advisory publication, *Capital Growth Letter*.

Our first study compared the bond average to the Bond Arms Index, calculated on a 10-day basis, in the standard manner. The results are shown in Figure 10–1. We can see at a glance that the highest point reached by the BAI10 at midyear coincides very closely with the low in the bond market, thereby indicating a buy point. The second highest point is also indicating a very good buying opportunity. There are, however, a number of other prominent peaks in the data, which, although they coincide well with the bottoms of dips, would not serve well as buy points because of the small magnitude of the subsequent moves. For example, by using the 1.20 level as a buy signal we would have six buy points during the year. The first two would lead to losses, the second two would be extremely good, and the last two would catch the bottoms of slight dips in the general advance. The problem is not with the index, but with the lack of volatility in the bond market. We are trying to find trading opportunities in a market that is too smooth to trade in such a short-term manner. It is evident, however, that the Bond Arms Index is

Figure 10–1

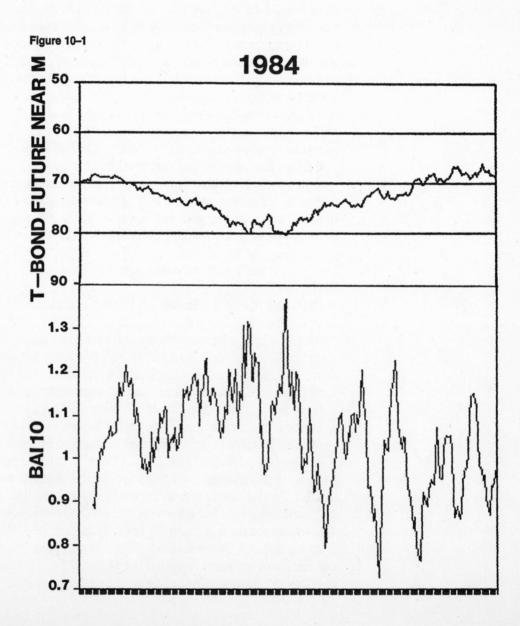

producing worthwhile information. We need to look at it correctly if we are to make good use of it.

The low points on the index should help us to find profit-taking sell opportunities. If we use the .80 level as a signal to sell, we find that there are three crossovers, all in the second half of the year. They do line up with high points in the bond index, but with minor highs which are soon exceeded. Evidently, as with stocks, the index is better on buys than on sells, or else we are looking at too short-term a picture, trying to be traders in a market which is not conducive to such activity.

Just to be sure we are not missing something, let us look at the open index rather than the standard calculation. Figure 10–2 shows that comparison, again on a 10-day basis. As we noticed in some of the prior work, the open index produces much sharper and more uniform peaks. Also, the overall values are somewhat lower. The most prominent peak still coincides with the best buy area, but now the other peaks are more nearly the same, making it harder to know the best opportunities. Using the 1.15 level as a signal would produce all the same signals

Figure 10–2

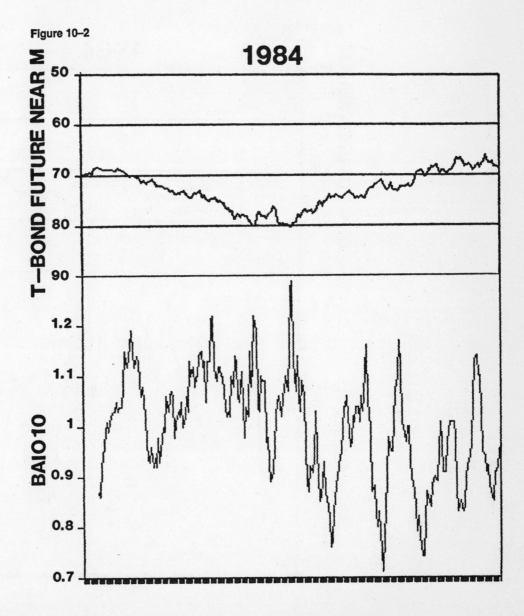

we saw in the standard calculation, with the same mediocre results. Similarly, the sell signals are in no way improved.

Obviously, it is going to be necessary to use a longer-term index. Figure 10–3 depicts the same period in the bond market, compared to a 21-day moving average of the BAI. Here, we begin to see much more useable results. The high in midyear is unmistakable and pinpoints the turn in interest rates. The lowest point in the BAI21 comes shortly before year-end, after the bond market has had a substantial advance. The market does continue to advance after the sell indication, however, making the signal seem early. Nevertheless, we are now seeing unequivocal signals which lead to profits. Looking at the lesser peaks and troughs in the index, we again find that they are of little value. Perhaps, therefore, we should go to an even less sensitive calculation and eliminate the extraneous gyrations.

Figure 10–4 shows almost four years of history and compares the bond market to a 55-day moving average of the BAI. The longer-term averaging has eliminated much of the whipsaw look to the index, and it has accentuated the longer-term

Figure 10–3

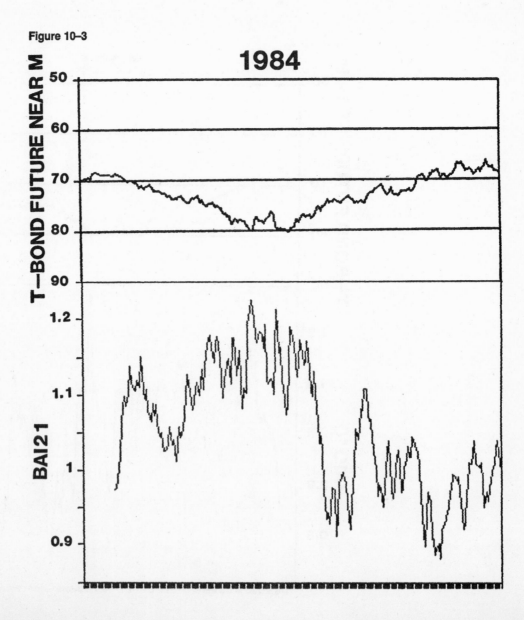

Figure 10-4

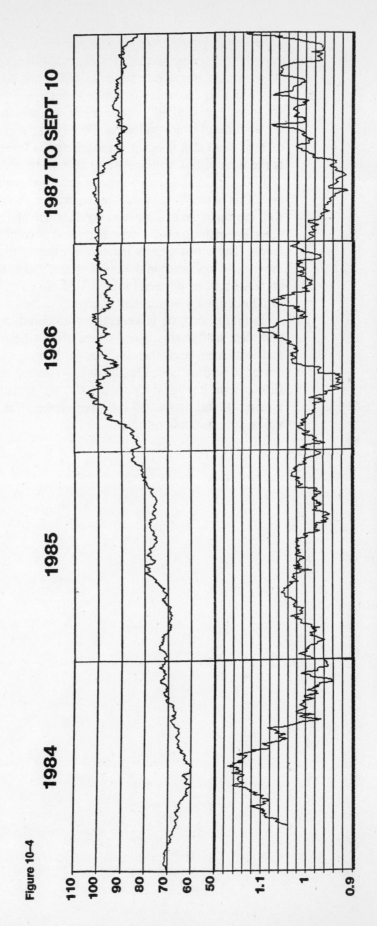

T—BOND FUTURES NEAR MONTH vs 55 DAY BOND ARMS INDEX

advances and declines. Now it is very apparent that there is an extremely close correlation between the index and the bond market. There is a major peak in 1984 which loudly broadcasts the news that the bond market is making an important low. No other move in the index reaches such heights. There are other peaks in the index, early in 1985 and in mid 1986, which point to buying opportunities at the bottoms of major pullbacks. Finally, at the edge of the chart in late September of 1987 the index is again approaching the levels of 1984. That buy signal has, at the time of this writing, yet to be proven right or wrong.

With this longer-term work we are now getting good results on the sell side also. One of the lowest points in the index is reached in early 1986, and it matches well the top of the bull move in bonds which had been going on for two years. The other low point comes a year later, and it coincides with the return to the same levels. These two signals indicate accurately the topping out of a major market move. The low point in the index in late 1984, which we noticed when studying the BAI21, is easily seen in the BAI55 also, and it proves to be a valid indication of an intermediate-term market top.

Technical analysis is generally considered in the province of equities rather than debt instruments. Bonds have always been regarded as more conservative and long-term, and, therefore, not a trading medium. In recent years this has ceased to be true, however. Bonds have moved enough to make them attractive as shorter-term holdings. Consequently, technicians would do well to apply their methods to this active and lucrative market. The BAI55 seems to provide a very valuable tool in this regard.

Chapter 11   Other Markets

Originally, the only data available for the calculation of an index was generated on the New York Stock Exchange. As a result, the original publications by not only the author, but other analysts, used that set of numbers. As use of the index spread, everyone continued to adopt the index, based on the NYSE as a proxy for the entire market. It is obvious, however, that all markets do not necessarily move together. Listed on the NYSE are usually the more seasoned companies, whereas most new issues start in the OTC market. The ASE has traditionally been the home of more speculative issues. Analysts have been aware for many years that bull moves tend to start with the highest quality stocks, and then to spread to the more speculative issues, so that the blue-chip sector is likely to top out long before the cats and dogs finish moving.

If exchanges tend to represent different market segments, and if each segment tends to behave differently in different market environments, shouldn't we then take a look at those other exchanges? The figures are now available, and have been for a number of years, which enable these calculations to be made. Moreover, since the beginning of 1987, Barrons has carried the calculated values for Arms Indices of the ASE and the OTC markets.

We have gone back and extracted the figures since the beginning of 1984, and calculated an Arms Index for both the American Stock Exchange and the Over-The-Counter markets. We then went one step further, combining all of these numbers into a single index which we will call, the Giant Arms Index, and abbreviate GAI. Figure 11–1 compares the results. We have, here, shown one year of history, and calculated a ten day moving average of the index for each exchange, and the Giant index, placing one above another.

The Giant Index is not an averaging of the individual calculated indices for each exchange. It is produced by adding the components before making the calculation. To get the giant advances we would add the advancing issues figures for the NYSE, the ASE and the OTC market. This would give us the first of the four numbers needed to make the index calculation. After developing the four components in this manner the index is calculated in the usual way.

Before doing these calculations we had expected to see the OTC index emerge as the most volatile, since it represented the most speculative market segment. We expected to see the ASE index is the next most volatile followed by the Giant Index, in that it contained these volatile segments. Our logic told us that the NYSE index would be the least volatile, since it contained more blue-chip stocks.

Surprise! We were completely wrong. The most volatile was the ASE, followed next by the NYSE, then the OTC, and finally the Giant. The reason is simple; volatility of the index is less dependent upon the speculative nature of the components than it is upon the size of the sample. Since the sum of the advances and declines on the ASE usually comes to about 600 issues, a single issue can have a more dramatic effect on the index than it could within a larger universe. Both the OTC market and the NYSE usually have about 1600 stocks represented in the sum of their advances and declines. Consequently, their index volatility is quite similar. The Giant index consists of all three markets, so its sum of advances and declines is usually about 3800 issues. Being such a large sample, the volatility of the index is by far the lowest.

As we compare the lines on Figure 11–1, it is apparent that the peaks and troughs are very nearly the same, although the amplitudes are different. This points out the fact that markets do move in concert. Regardless of the exchange, market tops and bottoms occur at the same time, and those tops and bottoms are clearly indicated by the index in each case. If this is true, then, why bother to follow any index besides the NYSE we are accustomed to? There are two reasons, compatibility and reliability.

Figure 11–1

1984

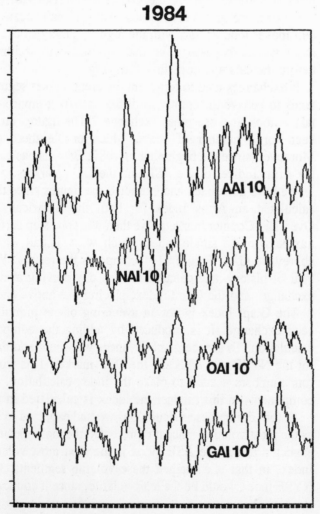

By compatibility we mean that we would like to use an index which is measuring the same stocks we are trading. If our investments are in the OTC market, we should be following an OTC indicator, since it is more likely to reflect the dynamics of that market. Figure 11–2 depicts the AAI10 plotted with the American Exchange market value index. Notice the extremely high peak in the AAI10 in mid-year. This coincides quite well with the lows in the market at that time. What is important, however, is the fact that ASE stocks made much lower lows than did the other exchanges. The blue chips were not as badly hit in that particular decline. The Arms indices for the other exchanges did not make such dramatic peaks. The AAI10 was evidently telling a different story; a story which only applied to that exchange. In this case, a compatible indicator is helpful, and it justifies keeping separate statistics for each exchange.

As we have seen, the size of the sample effects volatility. It also seems to effect reliability. In Figure 11–3 we see the way in which the Giant Arms Index relates to the broad market. We have used the Wilshire 5000 as a companion for the GAI10, since it is measuring approximately the same universe. Notice that the peaks and troughs of the GAI10 coincide very well with the tops and bottoms in

Figure 11–2

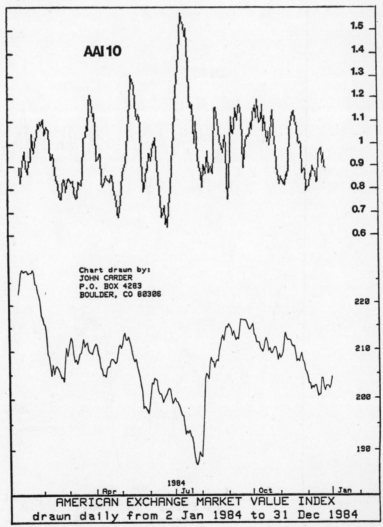

the market. Each high in the index correctly forecasts a subsequent advance in the market. Going back to the price chart, Figure 11–2, the results are not as reliable. Signals are often early and are sometimes erroneous. Evidently, the larger sample of data used in the Giant Index produces more reliable results. This, we believe, justifies the effort of following and calculating the extra indicator.

In these examples, for the sake of uniformity and simplicity, we have used 10-day moving averages of each index. Actually, any and all adaptations covered in prior chapters relating to the New York Stock Exchange Arms Index are equally useful on the other exchanges. Figure 11–4 shows the GAI21-GAI55 crossovers for the year 1985. We can see that we still are able to determine future market direction by the crossovers, just as we did in the NAI work.

At the present time it is still difficult to get the information on the ASE and OTC advancing and declining figures and volume statistics. This makes it somewhat difficult to follow these as closely as we do the NYSE index. The

Figure 11–3

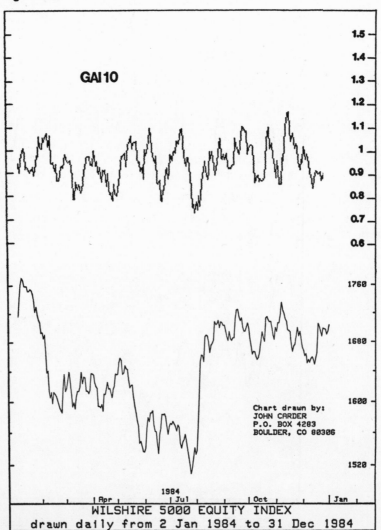

Figure 11–4

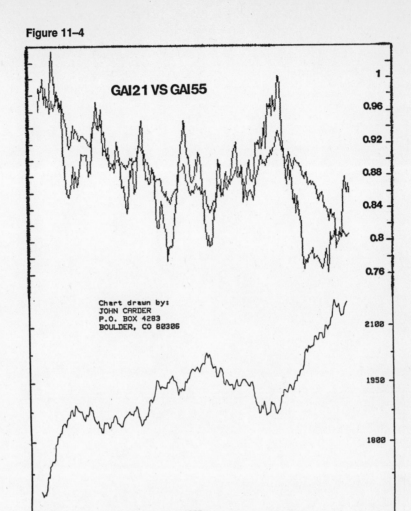

NYSE statistics are readily available on all quotation systems. Consequently, most investors will probably need to concentrate on the NYSE results even when trading other markets. At the end of each week the figures appear in *Barron's*, however, and we would suggest gathering this data if a person wishes to zero in better on other markets.

Chapter 12   Intermarket Comparisons

Having developed indices for other markets besides the traditional NYSE, one begins to observe how they compare to one another and wonder if they can be of help in making better market decisions. In that they represent rather different markets, it would be expected that they would show individual characteristics.

The first thing to look for would be lead time. We know that typical bull markets show a rotation of groups and a progression from conservative issues to speculative issues as the move progresses. This is a longer-term phenomenon, however. Perhaps, though, there is a similar effect on a shorter-term basis, where the more speculative issues make tops and bottoms later than the blue chips. If so, we would expect the peaks on the NYSE to come a little earlier than those on the ASE or OTC indices. Strangely enough, the opposite seems to be the case. Looking back to the first illustration of the prior chapter (Figure 11–1) we see that the top line, the AAI0, almost always reaches its maximums and minimums a few days before the other indices. Evidently, moves terminate sooner on the more speculative issues. This appears to be an important observation. It means that we should follow and remain alert to changes in direction in the ASE Arms Index, even if we are not trading ASE stocks. It can alert us to an imminent change in direction in the other exchanges.

In comparing the other three lines on the chart we are somewhat surprised, also, to see that the NYSE and OTC indices do not seem to lead or lag one another. The Giant index does not impart any additional information either.

The other obvious difference between the indices is their amplitude. As we noticed before, the ASE is most volatile, with the other indices much smoother. We tried overlaying these indices to see if there was any validity to the supposition that the more volatile index would show its widest divergence from the less volatile index at tops and bottoms. We reasoned that speculative excesses at turning points would show up more strongly in the ASE, moving that index away from its more sedate counterparts.

We found that there seemed to be an excellent correlation in some cases, but were bothered by the cluttered nature of our graphics. Asking the computer to plot the two lines resulted in a confusing crisscrossing of very similar plots. To remedy this, we first subtracted one column of numbers from the other, and then we plotted the results on a bar chart. This gave us a series of bars above and below the center line, as in Figure 12–1.

This plot is the difference between the NAI10 and the AAI10. Where the plot is above the line, the AAI10 was higher than the NAI10, and vice versa. One can

Figure 12-1

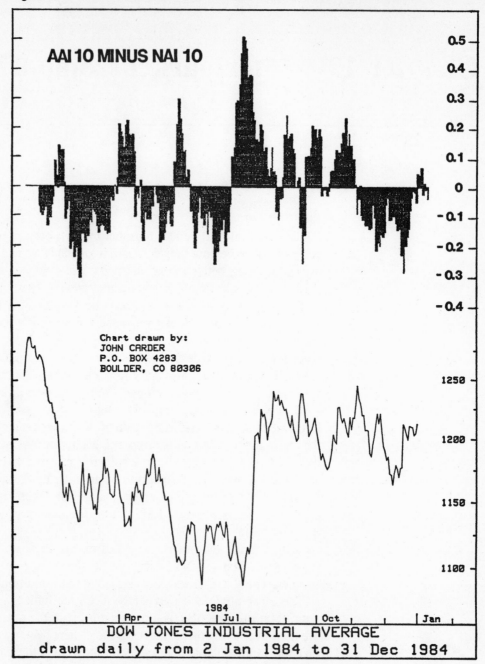

see that the areas of plots above the center line seem to be periods when one would want to be long in the market, and that the areas below the centerline coincide with times one would want to be short. Beyond that, however, the indicator ceases to be helpful. There are too many whipsaws, indicating we are looking at too short a time span, and some signals are disasterously wrong. Interesting results, but not something on which to risk your life's savings.

We decided to follow the same procedure, but lengthen the time frame to 21-day indices. The result is shown in Figure 12–2. Here we are getting somewhat smoother results with fewer whipsaws. Again, the areas above the line are areas when one would like to be long, and the areas below the line are periods

Figure 12–2

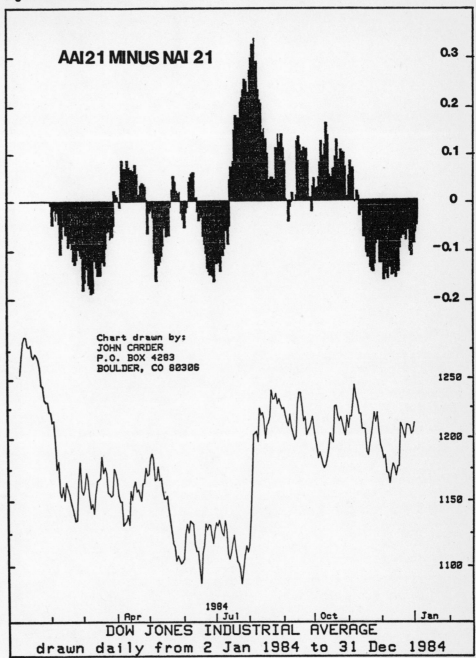

when one would like to be short. Even here, however, we feel that the correlation is too uncertain to serve as a trading tool. It could be used as a confirming indication, however. If one was long and saw that the AAI21 had gone to a very large premium over the NAI21, it would be a warning that things were getting overdone. One would be alerted that some profit taking might be in order.

We also ran comparisons matching the other indices to one another, using various time frames. Suffice it to say that the results were in all cases less satisfactory than those using the AAI and NAI.

It would appear that the comparison of one exchange Arms Index to another is most useful in observing lead times, and less useful, but somewhat significant, in recognizing excesses in the marketplace.

Chapter 13   Weighted Moving Averages

In all of the foregoing examinations of the Arms Index, when we have used moving averages we have given equal weight to all of the components of the moving average. For example, in a 5-day moving average, the data from 5 days ago was considered to be as important as today's information, yet the next day it was dropped entirely and was deemed useless. On a 55-day moving average, all of those 55 days were considered equally important, no matter how long ago they occurred, and were given equal strength in our moving average.

It is logical, however, to apply weighting to the moving averages. Today, being more immediate, would seem to have more importance in predicting tomorrow or next week, than would data from trading three months ago. On the other hand, just throwing away the older data and using a very short-term moving average has the effect of producing a very volatile index. By weighting the data we can retain the older data, but relegate it to a progressively smaller role as it becomes less immediate. The effect should be an index which is more sensitive than an equal-length, nonweighted average but smoother than a shorter-term, non-weighted average.

There are two ways of weighting the results; arithmetic and exponential. The results are essentially the same, but the method of calculation is different. In an arithmetic calculation a weighting is assigned to each component. For example, if we were doing a 5-day weighted moving average of the Arms Index, the calculation might go as below.

	AI		weight		weighted value
4 days ago	.85	×	1	=	.85
3 days ago	.75	×	2	=	1.50
2 days ago	1.32	×	3	=	3.96
Yesterday	1.12	×	4	=	4.48
Today	1.05	×	5	=	5.25
			15		16.04/15 = 107

We see, then, that the weighted 5-day moving average for that day is 1.07.

The weighting can be varied in any number of ways. The time span can be lengthened or shortened, and the degree of weighting can be varied. For example, we could have multiplied the closer information by larger numbers and the earlier information by smaller numbers in order to emphasize the recent information even more.

Exponential moving averages have the advantage that one does not need to retain as much information, nor make such lengthy calculations. A value is placed on today's data, and it is then affixed to yesterday's data, which has been similarly valued on a percentage basis. We could, for example, decide to give today 10 percent of the weighting and yesterday 90 percent of the weighting. If we have been making this calculation day after day, for some time, then yesterday's data contains the weighted value of the days which preceded it, yet we never have to go back and look at those days again.

A disadvantage to this method of weighting is our inability to heavily overweight current data as we could in the arithmetic weighting. In addition, there is a tendency to be somewhat misled by the fact that one can have immediate results using this method. On only the second day of calculation one has a number which looks legitimate even though the moving average may have been designed to encompass many weeks of trading. In reality, the previous day, being the only information available, is getting too much weight. One must be aware of this and not start to believe the readings until a reasonable amount of data is accumulated.

In the examples which follow we will be talking about days, not percentages. We will look, for example, at a 10-day exponential moving average of the index. Actually, this means that we will be weighting today's index at 18 percent of the total, and yesterday's calculated value at 82 percent of the value. The formula for converting number of days to percentage weighting is: $\% = 2/(\text{days} + 1)$

In Figure 13–1 we compare the 10-day moving average of the index using the three methods of calculation; the unweighted moving average, the arithmetically weighted moving average, and the exponentially weighted moving average. It is immediately apparent that the weighted and the exponential plots are almost identical. On close scrutiny one can see a few small differences, but not differences which would in any way change one's interpretation of the chart. On the other hand, the unweighted moving average is quite different from the other two. In general, the unweighted is somewhat smoother, and the turning points are more rounded. The small swings are less pronounced, giving a slightly less confusing picture. There are two very important differences, however. One is the timing of each individual signal, and the other is the difference in double tops and double bottoms in the index.

Because of the accentuation of recent information, the weighted indices tend to be somewhat earlier in giving signals. If one places a straight-edge on Figure 13–1 and equates similar points, such as those lettered A through E, it will be seen that the signals are usually a few days earlier on the weighted indices. Relating these points to the position of the market at the time (see the market chart at the top of Figure 13–2), it works out to be more profitable to act just a little bit sooner than would be possible using the unweighted index.

At point B, especially, one sees the difference between the double tops in the two methods. In the weighted index, the first top is higher and more pronounced than is the second. On the unweighted index the second top is more pronounced. In most cases, we have found, the unweighted index gives a better signal because the weighted first peak is at a less important turning point than is the second. It appears, then, that the score is tied. The weighted index is better at timing, being slightly earlier, and the unweighted is better in major turns where double signals are given. This suggests we should, if possible, keep our eye on both calculations.

That was the 10-day, a rather short-term indicator. What about longer-term calculations? Is there any advantage to using a weighted moving average on

Figure 13–1

1975

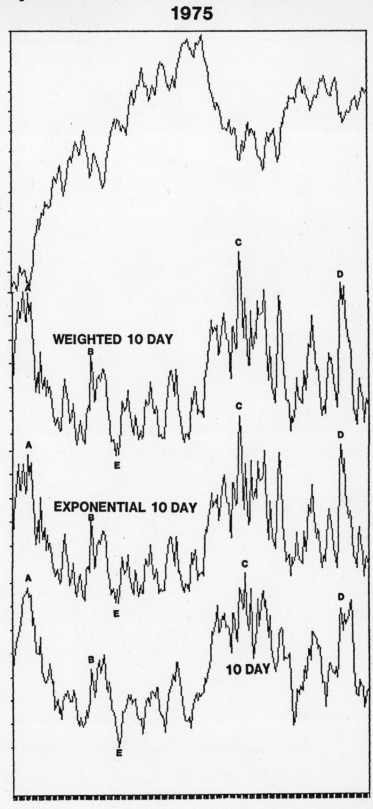

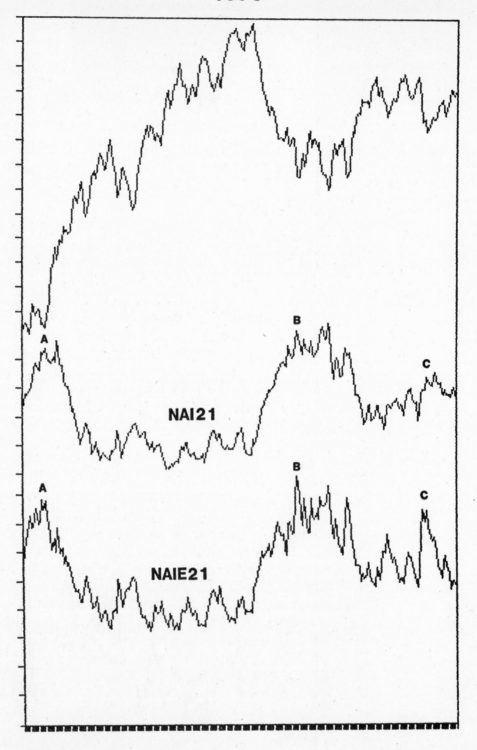

Figure 13–2

1975

Figure 13–3

1975·1976·1977

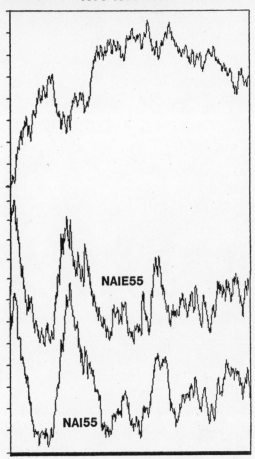

NAIE55

NAI55

these? In Figure 13–2 we are again looking at the same time period, but now we are relating it to the 21-day index. The center line on the chart is the unweighted 21-day index (NAI21), and the lower line is the exponentially weighted 21-day index, (NAIE21). Again, as in the 10-day, it is apparent that the weighted index produces sharper peaks and more gyrations. Unlike the earlier work, however, there seems to be little difference in timing. The peaks and troughs on the two indices coincide nicely. On the other hand, we are now seeing better signals from the weighted moving average when multiple tops are made. At point A the weighted average gave a much more timely buy signal than did the unweighted. At point B either signal served equally well, while at point C the weighted index gave a much stronger indication it was time to buy. We feel that a weighted 21-day index can be helpful and justifies the extra labor.

Finally, let us go way out to a 55-day plot. Because we are interested in longer-term moves we have covered three years in Figure 13–3 rather than just one. Again, the difference in volatility can be seen. Other than that, however, the two lines are very similar. Both are very helpful in finding the major market bottoms, and both do a fairly good job of indicating market tops. In this respect the unweighted index may be somewhat better. We feel that either indicator can be used, achieving quite similar results.

Chapter 14   Other Techniques

The different approaches to the use of the index fall into two categories: mathematical variations and time variations. We have tried to cover a large number of time variations, and apply them to the various techniques we have discussed, such as the open index, the weighted index, etc. However, the number of time variations is limitless. There are those who swear by a 30-day average, others who use a weighted 20-day, and some who prefer a very long average such as the 100-day index.

It appears, in talking to each of these people, that the usefulness of the index is largely based upon a person's familiarity with that particular method. Basically, the index, in its raw form, is measuring the underlying pressures of the marketplace. On a short-term basis it recognizes shifts in investor sentiment; on a longer-term basis it recognizes overbought and oversold conditions. From that point, all mathematical juggling of the numbers is meant to make the information more easily understood. The numbers themselves remain unchanged. Therefore, if a person feels comfortable with a particular method, and studies it closely, he will begin to feel that it is the best method; he understands it.

We have tried to cover a large number of different calculations, but are aware we too have our prejudices, and they are probably based at least partially on familiarity. We urge the reader to try his own calculations in order to be comfortable with the results. This should lead to the making of better market decisions.

One interesting method of smoothing is used by Ned Davis, of Ned Davis Research, Inc. in Venice, Florida. He smooths the data for each day, prior to constructing his moving average. His first step is to average the value of the Arms Index for two readings during the day; 1:00 PM and 4:00 PM New York time. Next, he constructs a 40-day moving average of those numbers. Finally, he places buy and sell signal lines at the .92 and .98 levels. This creates a very narrow neutral zone. On any move above .98 he is a buyer, and on any move below .92 he is a seller. Based on these signals alone, he shows theoretical gains over a seven-year period, which do about 50 percent better than a buy-and-hold strategy using the Dow Jones Industrials as a proxy for the market.

The above work is interesting, and the results are impressive. We are a little bit bothered by the two readings per day from a mathematical standpoint. Information is being included twice, in that the 4:00 PM numbers contain the previously noted 1:00 PM information. However, if it makes money consistently, then why argue about the fine points of the calculations.

Another timing approach is particularly noteworthy for its simplicity and effectiveness. In Chapter 2 we pointed out that bullish days tend to be followed by bearish days, and vice versa. Moreover, two consecutive very bearish days are rather unusual and imply a market which is becoming oversold. Newton Zinder was one of the first people to recognize this, and he pointed to two days over 2.00 as a signal to buy. Two money managers, James Alphier of Argus Investment Management in Santa Barbara, California, and William Kuhn of Invest/O in Bend, Oregon, picked up on this and wondered if just one very bearish day was enough evidence to serve as a signal. Their article in *Stocks and Commodities* magazine in April 1987 shows their results.

They arbitrarily chose 2.65 as their breakpoint, and decided they would, theoretically, be buyers any time a single day's reading exceeded that level. Furthermore, they would automatically sell out eight months later. If another "over 2.65" index came along during the holding period, the clock was set back to zero for another eight-month holding period.

Their study covered over twenty years of market history and resulted in eleven different buys. Only one produced a loss, and that loss was extremely small. Overall, the market during that time was up 192.1 percent but their timing upped that to 441.1 percent. They would have been completely out of the market for more than half the time.

Often analysts combine the index with other indicators so that a signal must be confirmed by some other market measurement. Ned Davis, mentioned above, does this and helps his results. Another is Al Frank, publisher of *The Prudent Speculator* in Santa Monica, California. He uses the 10-day index, but requires that his buy-and-sell signals be confirmed by the Advance-Decline figures.

Arthur Merrill, of Merrill Analysis, Inc. in Chappaqua, NY, was probably the first analyst to invert the index, which really makes a lot of sense. It means that lows on the index match lows on the market, rather than the other way around as it now is calculated. Unfortunately, by the time anyone realized the index was going to be so popular it was too late to invert it. It had become a part of Wall Street methodology in its less logical form. Anyone wishing to correct this only has to swap the positions of the denominator and the numerator in the original equation. If the index has already been calculated, take the reciprocal of each value, (1/Arms Index).

From time to time in prior chapters we have referred to the fact that the index is affected by being restricted in the direction of small numbers, but not in the direction of large numbers. Over the years a number of mathematicians have devised esoteric ways of dealing with this. However, the very simple solution, for those bothered by this quirk, was suggested by John McGinley, of *Technical Trends*. Simply plot the information on a log scale rather than an arithmetic scale. We did this in the chapter dealing with intraday swings. It is in the shortest-term calculations that such an adjustment may be desirable. As longer-term moving averages are applied to the work the distortion ceases to be a problem.

One should realize that we are not in any way changing the numbers, we are only plotting them on semi-log paper in order to see the information more clearly. The log plot spreads out the low numbers and compresses the high numbers. This makes the extreme lows a little more apparent and brings down the dramatic peaks in the large numbers.

Chapter 15   Sources of Data

If one is to make use of the material in this book, it will be necessary to keep up with the information. There are three parts to this task: first, one must have access to current information; secondly, one must have a backlog of historical data with which to compare the current information; and third, one must have a way of displaying the information.

On a daily basis there is really very little data needed in order to keep up with the index. If one only wants to follow the New York Stock Exchange Arms Index, a quick call to a broker after the market close should yield the various components. It will be necessary to get all the numbers; the advances, the declines, the advancing volume, and the declining volume, if the open index is to be calculated. Otherwise, it is even easier. Most quotation systems carry the index already calculated. From there on it is simply a lot of labor computing the moving averages.

It is also possible to get the figures the next morning from *The Wall Street Journal*. Don't look for the computed index though, it isn't there; you'll have to do your own calculation. In addition, the financial sections of many other newspapers carry the same numbers.

The Financial News Network is a very easy way of getting the information. Long after the market has closed, the value for the index will continue to cross the tape on your television screen every few minutes. Again, however, this is only the NYSE index. In addition, other financial television channels usually carry the index, generally still using the TRIN designation.

In order the get the daily values for the American Stock Exchange and the Over-the-Counter Arms indices, it will be necessary to collect the data and make the calculations, since, to the best of our knowledge, no service provides daily calculated values. *Barron's* does provide the daily values, but not until the end of the week. That means being behind on the information much of the time. The values can be found in the "Market Laboratory" section, under the heading "Arms Index." In addition, the components are printed in another part of the same section.

Each day *The Wall Street Journal* carries the advance-decline figures and the advancing volume-declining volume figures, not only for the NYSE but also for the ASE and OTC markets as well. These are usually on the inside of the last page. The Giant Arms Index, is, of course, computed from these numbers, but is not calculated and displayed in any periodical.

We have only found one source, so far, for the necessary data for the Bond Arms Index. This is a data-base service provided by Hale Systems, Inc.

In the work dealing with intraday uses of the index, we suggested watching the index closely and plotting the changes versus the changing Dow Industrials throughout the trading day. In order to do this, and we do recommend it as a way of becoming familiar with the index, it will be necessary to be close to a source of information. Perhaps the easiest way is through watching the tape on the Financial News Network during the trading day. The current index is recalculated and displayed on the screen continuously. This makes the job of monitoring quite easy. An alternative is to sit in a brokerage office and periodically check the index and the market on a quote machine.

If one wishes to monitor standard charts of the index, both open and normal calculations, such information is available through a number of market-charting services, both in hard-copy form and as dial-up computer information. We particularly like the home computer charts put out by Computer Asset Management, in Salt Lake City. In chapter 11 we made use of some custom-produced charts of various market indices. These were provided by John Carder, who can provide many similar charts of the index plotted in various ways. Many advisory letters occasionally print charts of the index, but these will, of course, be the favorite applications of the writer of the advisory letter.

Assuming one elects to keep his own data rather than subscribe to a chart service or various newsletters, the historical data is available in printed form or as computer information from a large number of data bases. Most will only have the components, not the calculated index, and some will not have the data for the other exchanges.

Owners of home computers who would like to closely follow all of the indices mentioned in this book can continuously access the raw data and the many computed values through a service offered by Arms-Equivolume Corporation, P.O. Box 53566, Albuquerque, NM, 87153. Included is 20 years of NYSE Arms Index historical data on floppy disks, and shorter histories for other exchanges.

In preparing this book, we found a small home computer to be invaluable. With a minimum amount of hardware, and using Lotus 1-2-3 software, we were able to look at hundreds of applications in graphic form. Many of these graphs were then modified for inclusion as illustrations. We suggest that any serious market participant consider using the same approach. Any good spreadsheet program will make the calculation of moving averages, open indices, weighted averages, and exponentially weighted averages extremely simple. Then, a good graphics program will turn the data into understandable displays.

The alternative is the hand calculation of indices and averages. We have done it for years, and we continue to make some simple calculations by hand on a daily basis. It is certainly a more difficult, but less expensive, approach. In addition, hand calculations give one a much better feel for the changes. We are all for automation. It removes a great deal of the dog work, but with the simplicity and speed comes a blind acceptance and often a loss of understanding. Even a person with the best computer equipment should occasionally do some work by hand, in order to appreciate more fully the meaning of the numbers.

Chapter 16   Conclusions

It is interesting that an index as simple to compute and understand as the Arms Index should provide enough material for an entire book. Perhaps it is just that simplicity which accounts for the wealth of additional work that has been done. The index measures such a fundamental balance in the marketplace, the interrelation of price and volume, that the applications are almost endless.

Among those many applications, we have, in the foregoing pages, arrived at a few which we feel are the most helpful. The market participant should first decide the category which best fits his investment aims, his temperament and his financial resources. Then he should use the appropriate indices to help to guide him in his quest for profits. This is not to say that other methods should be ignored, since all information can be helpful; but a long-term trader, for example, should not be overly concerned with the action of the intraday moves except when he is actually establishing or liquidating positions. At that time, of course, he should use any means available in order to trade at the best prices. This means temporarily becoming very aware of minor moves.

For the very long-term investor, his best indicator will be the extremely oversold and overbought conditions which are best seen in the 55-day moving average of the index. If, for example, the 1.30 level had been used as a buy point over the last twenty years, he would have been a buyer only three times; 1970, 1974 and 1987. All of these would have led to a participation in extremely profitable bull moves. By then selling the position when the AI55 went below .85 the 1970 move would have produced a profitable participation in a market advance which exceeded 50 percent and was accomplished in less than three years. The 1974 bottom would have led to a sell signal about three years later and a move in the market of over 60 percent. The results of the 1987 buy, immediately after the October panic, are not yet clear at the time of this writing, but the market has moved up sharply from those lows.

For the long-term investor, the same indicator may be used but the parameters should be narrowed to generate more trades. This still allows participation in major market moves, but also helps with the somewhat shorter swings. By buying when the NAI55 exceeds 1.20 and selling when it drops below .90 many more trades are initiated, trades which lead to consistent profits.

Intermediate-term traders should concentrate on the 21-55 crossovers. We have followed and used this for many years, and we have been able to recognize most important market moves, on both the upside and the downside. This methodology has the advantage of two indices, thereby adjusting the parameters for the kind of market currently in existence. It means many more trades, of course, and constant market participation. The two longer-term approaches cited above produce many long periods when one is entirely out of the market.

For those with the interest and fortitude to withstand the emotional pressure of short-term trading, we feel the 4-13 relationship, with the 15 percent spread, as explained in chapter 7, is the most effective. Of course, as one moves to shorter time spans, the potential for quickly compounding principal becomes much larger, but so does the risk.

One should, however, continue to follow other applications as well as the primary application which fits one's form of trading. As we have seen, there are clues found in other markets, in other moving averages, in the open calculations, in the very long-term averages, and in the daily figures. None of these should be ignored if they can help one to reach more effective market decisions.

We often receive letters which reflect people's continuing suspicion of the underpinnings of this index. They usually reflect a concern over the observation that the index can be bearish when the market is bullish, and vice versa. Particularly disconcerting is a day in which there are many more stocks up than down, producing a strong advance-decline reading, yet the index is over 1.00 because the volume did not show such strength.

We like to answer this question with an analogy. Suppose your family consists of a dozen children, half boys and half girls. You are going to give out chocolate-chip cookies to these children. Each girl will receive three cookies, while each boy will only receive two cookies. An observer will see that all of your children are eating cookies and believe that you are being very fair, favoring neither the boys nor the girls. A closer look, however, tells a different story. The girls are evidently your favorites; they are getting 50 percent more cookies. The index of cookies shows six girls getting cookies and six boys getting cookies; a standoff. The volume-adjusted cookie index shows the favoritism which was not evident without the closer scrutiny. A volume cookie index, from the standpoint of the girls, would be .67, a very bullish reading.

The other point which occasionally is bothersome is the fact that low numbers on a short-term basis are good (bullish), yet on a long-term basis those same low numbers become bad (bearish). Our explanation is that the market cannot stand too much of a good thing. It is much like our foregoing example of cookie-eating children. On a short-term basis the extra ration of cookies is good for the girls. If you continue to dole out the cookies in this proportion for very long though, pretty soon the girls are going to get overfed and perhaps sick. They have been given too many cookies for too long.

So it is with the market. If the advancing stocks are receiving more than their share of the volume, they are being favored by investors; a bullish sign. If this continues for very long, however, the advancing stocks become overfed and get sick. They will have to stop eating until they lose some weight and regain their appetites.

It is this relationship which makes the index valuable. It measures the amount of volume going to each side of the market. On a short-term basis, it indicates the favoritism of the investors, a favoritism which may not be observable if one ignores volume. On a longer-term basis, it recognizes situations wherein the favoritism has persisted for so long that it is no longer maintainable. It spots the children who have eaten too much and are likely to get sick.

That underlying validity then leads to the myriad of methodologies. We have attempted to cover many of them in the foregoing pages, but the quest is not over. Perhaps a thorough testing will reveal other divisors which give better results than the ones we have suggested. There may be weighting methods which are more effective. This book is not the final word, it is a series of suggestions and a few guideposts for further exploration. We hope that others will continue to look for better methods, and we sincerely urge that those methods be made available to the public by their developers.

Index

D1061228